Countdown to Spanish GCSE

A ten-day revision workbook to prepare you for the exam

About the author

Lucy Martin was educated in Brussels and the UK and has a first-class degree in Modern Languages from Wadham College, Oxford. She speaks five languages and teaches to all levels, with a superb track record in top exam results. She is a contributor to BBC Bitesize and has written twelve books of her own for students of French, Spanish and German. She lives in London with her three children.

www.lucymartintuition.co.uk

Table of contents

This book is dedicated to every single one of you taking GCSE or IGCSE Spanish this year. Good luck!

Introduction

I produced this book in response to demand from students and parents looking for a day by day revision and study guide. There are plenty of grammar and vocabulary books on the market, but there was definitely a call for something that could be studied in bitesize chunks and was not too overwhelming in terms of content.

The ten chapters take you through all the essentials of the GCSE syllabus in terms of grammar, vocabulary and oral answers, with a special section at the end on tips and strategies for the listening and writing papers. So rather than spend a whole day learning vocabulary, you focus on a few grammar points followed by exercises on those points, then a short vocabulary list and oral questions and answers that relate to the grammar and vocabulary of the day.

I have limited it to ten chapters so that it is a manageable task for the Christmas holidays (before the mock exams) or the Easter holidays (before the main exams). There is a fair bit of material in each chapter, so depending on your current level, you may take a couple of hours to complete the work in each. Ideally, you complete the book once at Christmas and then again at Easter, by which time it should be a much faster process.

Don't forget that you can also watch the videos on my Lucy Martin Tuition YouTube channel which will help you get through the oral and the writing by focusing on standard impressive answers that you can adapt to suit individual questions. These standard answers are in this book in text boxes.

Finally, I am always keen to hear from my readers and fellow teachers and tutors. Please don't hesitate to get in touch via my website www.lucymartintuition.co.uk

NOTES

Day 1

In this session you will be revising:

- Nouns, gender and articles
- Adjectives and their agreements
- Regular verbs in the present tense
- Infinitives and how to use them
- Vocabulary relating to family and general topics
- Oral and written answers on describing people

Gender

Spanish nouns are masculine or feminine. Generally the ones that end in *a* are feminine and the rest are masculine.

El teatro   the theatre (masculine)

La biblioteca   the library (feminine)

Un cine   a cinema (masculine)

Una casa   a house (feminine)

but there are a few exceptions!

Nouns ending in -*ma* are masculine

el problema, el programa, el tema (theme), el dilema

Some nouns ending in *a* are masculine

el día, el mapa, el sofá, el planeta.

Words ending in -*tion* in English end in -*ción* in Spanish and they are all feminine

reservación, conversación, contaminación, acción, atención, colaboración, clasificación, colección, combinación, concentración, condición, construcción, nación, operación, discriminación

Words ending in -*ty* in English end in -*dad* in Spanish and they are all feminine

universidad, sociedad, ciudad, calidad / cualidad (quality), capacidad, comunidad, curiosidad, dificultad, cantidad (quantity), velocidad, diversidad, creatividad, celebridad, variedad, publicidad

Articles

Definite articles

There are 4 words for "the" in Spanish depending on whether the noun is masculine or feminine and singular or plural:

el perro	the dog
los perros	the dogs
la chica	the girl
las chicas	the girls

Use them as you would use *the* in English, and also when expressingwhat you like and don't like (*me gustan los perros / prefiero el chocolate*). Also remember that when you're talking about something in general (eg, dogs are boring) you will need an article in Spanish (*los perros son aburridos*).

Indefinite articles

There are two words for "a" depending on whether the noun is masculine or feminine:

un gato	a cat
una mesa	a table

Add an "s" or "os" for "some"

unos coches	some cars
unas chicas	some girls

You don't need an indefinite article when you are talking about jobs.

Quiero ser professor	I want to be a teacher
Mi madre es enfermera	My mother is a nurse

Test yourself on these

the library	la biblioteca
the table	la mesa
the houses	las casas
a cat	un gato
some conversations	unas conversaciones
the reservation	la reservación
a city	una ciudad
a theatre	un teatro
the university	la universidad
a car	un coche
the girls	las chicas
a boy	un chico
some tables	unas mesas
a society	una sociedad
a cinema	un cine
the cinemas	los cines
a library	una biblioteca
a house	una casa
cats are fun	los gatos son divertidos
I am studying French	estudio el francés
I like trains	me gustan los trenes
I hate the rain	odio la lluvia

Verbs in the present tense

Conjugating a verb means adapting it to the person who is doing it. In English, present tense conjugation is mostly straightforward. We keep the verb the same whoever is doing it, except that with the he/she/it form we add an s *(I eat, you eat, he/she eats, we eat, you eat, they eat)*.

We need to conjugate verbs in Spanish, but we don't need to include the pronoun. The ending of the verb tells you who is doing it. So, for example, if you see a *"mos"* on the end of a verb, the person who is doing it is going to be "we". *"Visitamos"* means *"we visit"*.

Although you don't have to use the pronouns (I, you, he, she, it, we, they), it is sometimes useful to know them for the purposes of your understanding, and for clarity or emphasis:

yo	I
tú	you (singular)
él	he
ella	she
usted	you (singular polite form)
nosotros	we
vosotros	you (plural)
ellos	they (masculine or mixed group)
ellas	they (feminine group)
ustedes	you (plural polite form)

You will notice a few things about this list. Firstly, there are two words for *"they"* depending on whether the group referred to is exclusively feminine or not.

Secondly, they have the polite "you" form that we don't have in English. In this book I am only using the familiar *"tú"* form, but the polite form is conjugated exactly like the *el / ella* form, or the *ellos / ellas* form depending on whether it is singular or plural.

Finally, the accents on tú and él are there to differentiate these words from the words tu (your) and el (the), and clarify meaning.

Three types of verbs in the present tense

Type 1 verbs ending in *-ar*

Hablar   **to speak**

Hablo	I speak
Hablas	you (singular) speak
Habla	he, she or it speaks
Hablamos	we speak
Habláis	you (plural) speak
Hablan	they speak

Type 2 verbs ending in *-er*

Comer   **to eat**

Como	I eat
Comes	you (singular) eat
Come	he, she or it eats
Comemos	we eat
Coméis	you (plural) eat
Comen	they eat

Type 3 verbs ending in *-ir*

Vivir   **to live**

Vivo	I live
Vives	you (singular) live
Vive	he, she or it lives
Vivimos	we live
Vivís	you (plural) live
Viven	they live

The **I** form ends in an *o*, the **he** form ends in *a/e*, the **we** form ends in *mos* and the **they** form always ends in an *n*.

Test yourself on these

hablan	they speak
viven	they live
vive	he/she lives
come	he/she eats
comemos	we eat
hablamos	we speak
hablo	I speak
vivo	I live
vivimos	we live
escuchan	they listen to
habla	he/she speaks
visito	I visit
aprendo	I learn
escuchamos	we listen to
aprenden	they learn
reciclamos	we recycle
habláis	you (pl) speak
visitamos	we visit
estudian	they study
visitan	they visit
comen	they eat
reciclo	I recycle
estudio	I study
aprendemos	we learn
escucho	I listen to
reciclan	they recycle
como	I eat
reservan	they reserve
comunicamos	we communicate
causa	he, she, it causes
uso	I use
preparas	you prepare
reservamos	we reserve
vivimos	we live
usan	they use
estudias	you study
visitáis	you (pl) visit

The verb *ser*

There are two verbs *to be* in Spanish – *ser* and *estar*. We use the verb *ser* to describe characteristics. This is how it goes:

soy	I am
eres	you are
es	he or she is
somos	we are
sois	you (pl) are
son	they are

Adjectives

Adjectives usually go after the noun and will agree with it in gender and number. This means that if the adjective ends in an *o*, it changes to an *a* if the noun it describes is feminine. If it ends in *-or* this changes to *-ora,* and they all get an extra *s* on the end (*-es* in the case of the ones ending in *-or*) if the noun they describe is plural. Adjectives ending in *e* like *inteligente* can't change to *a*, so they only agree in number. *Deportista* doesn't change in the singular at all. *Mucho, demasiado* and *todo* count as adjectives and must agree with the noun they describe.

Un perro grande, blanco y español – a big white Spanish dog

Unos chicos son deportistas – some boys are sporty

Unas chicas graciosas – some funny girls

Much**as** personas – lots of people

Tod**a** la familia – all the family

Todos los días – every day

Todo el tiempo – all the time

Todas las manzanas – all the apples

Hay demasiad**os** deberes – there is too much homework

Possessive adjectives

Possessive adjectives go in front of the noun they refer to and only agree in number in the singular forms. So, the word for *my* when we say *my sister* (mi hermana) is different from when we say *my brothers* (mis hermanos). Here they all are:

mi hermano / hermana	my brother / sister
mis padres	my parents
tus hermanos / hermanas	your brothers / sisters
tus padres	your parents
su hermano / hermana	his, her or their brother / sister
sus padres	his, her or their parents
nuestro hermano	our brother
nuestros hermanos	our brothers
nuestra hermana	our sister
nuestras hermanas	our sisters
vuestro hermano	your (from you *pl*) brother
vuestros hermanos	your (from you *pl*) brothers
vuestra hermana	your (from you *pl*) sister
vuestras hermanas	your (from you *pl*) sisters

Test yourself on adjective agreements

Failure to agree adjectives is the most common mistake at GCSE and even A level, but such an easy one to avoid. In the exercise that follows, repeat until you can put all the sentences into Spanish. Concentrate not just on agreeing the adjectives but on getting the article (a/the) right and making the verb agree with the subject.

English	Spanish
1. We live in a yellow house	Vivimos en una casa amarilla
2. They live in my village	Viven en mi pueblo
3. The girl eats her sandwich	La chica come su bocadillo
4. We eat lots of pizza	Comemos mucha pizza
5. I sing all the time	Canto todo el tiempo
6. There is too much pollution	Hay demasiada contaminación
7. I eat all the oranges	Como todas las naranjas
8. His friend doesn't eat pasta	Su amigo no come pasta
9. There are good beaches in Spain	Hay playas buenas en España
10. The teachers are good	Los profesores son buenos
11. My parents are strict	Mis padres son estrictos
12. There are too many cars	Hay demasiados coches
13. The swimming pool is long	La piscina es larga
14. I work all day	Trabajo todo el día
15. Our parents are fun	Nuestros padres son divertidos
16. Your (s) mother is funny	Tu madre es graciosa
17. Your (pl) father is shy	Vuestro padre es tímido
18. Their friends are boring	Sus amigos son aburridos
19. I study modern history	Estudio historia moderna
20. Planes are fast	Los aviones son rápidos

Using infinitives

Spanish verbs are hard to conjugate. To avoid conjugating them, especially in the present tense where the irregular ones can trip you up, you can use one of these expressions followed by an infinitive:

1. **To say what you like and don't like – me gusta**

No me gusta trabajar	I don't like working
Me gusta dormir	I like sleeping

2. **To say what you usually do - suelo**

Suelo comer mucha fruta	I usually eat a lot of fruit
No suelo llegar tarde	I don't usually arrive late

3. **To say what you have to or can do – tengo que**

Tengo que salir	I have to go out
Tenemos que trabajar	We have to work
No tengo que ir	I don't have to go
No tenemos que escuchar	We don't have to listen

4. **To say what you can do – puedo**

¿Puedo venir?	Can I come?
¿Pueden salir?	Can they go out?
No puedo hacer mucho	I can't do much

5. **To say what you want to do – quiero**

Quiero comprar un bocadillo	I want to buy a sandwich
Quieren ir al cine	They want to go to the cinema

6. **To make the FUTURE TENSE – voy a + infinitive**

Voy a vivir en España	I am going to live in Spain
No voy a comer mucho	I am not going to eat much

Some high-frequency verbs to learn

Hablar	to speak
Comer	to eat
Vivir	to live
Ayudar	to help
Trabajar	to work
Viajar	to travel
Limpiar	to clean
Llevar	to wear or carry
Llegar	to arrive
Ir	to go
Hacer	to do
Poner	to put
Deber	to have to
Poder	to be able to
Recibir	to receive
Beber	to drink
Comprar	to buy
Ver	to watch
Dar	to give
Decir	to say
Escribir	to write
Empezar	to begin
Terminar	to finish
Abrir	to open
Cerrar	to close

Reciclar	to recycle
Usar	to use
Escuchar	to listen
Entender	to hear or understand
Comprender	to understand
Descansar	to relax
Jugar	to play
Conocer	to know
Encontrar	to meet
Perder	to lose
Buscar	to look for
Olvidar	to forget
Vender	to sell
Volver	to return
Apagar	to turn off
Ahorrar	to save
Descargar	to download
Ganar	to earn or win
Gastar	to spend
Malgastar	to waste
Asistir a	to attend
Charlar	to chat
Discutir	to argue
Cuidar	to look after
Pedir	to ask for

Important reflexive verbs – test yourself

Levantarse	to get up
Despertarse	to wake up
Ducharse	to shower
Vestirse	to get dressed
Divertirse	to have fun
Broncearse	to sunbathe
Alojarse	to stay (accommodation)
Quedarse	to stay (general)
Quejarse	to complain
Reunirse	to get together
Darse cuenta de que	to realise
Acostarse	to go to bed
Relajarse	to relax
Casarse	to get married
Separarse	to separate
Llevarse bien / mal con	to get on well / badly with

These verbs work like other verbs but you put the pronoun first

Me levanto	I get up
Te levantas	you get up
Se levanta	he / she gets up
Nos levantamos	we get up
Os levantáis	you (pl) get up
Se levantan	they get up

Adding to infinitives

Here are some useful additions to those infinitives

Jugar al futbol / tenis / golf – to play football/tennis/golf

The rule of thumb is that when you play something – use *al* before the sport or game, and they are mostly the same word as English (cricket, hockey, rugby) but sometimes with a more phonetic spelling – *voleibol, tenis, netbol.*

Hacer deporte – to do sport

We don't "play" sport, we do it. It's the same with all non-ball sports: you *hacer* most of them – *jogging, ciclismo, vela, patinaje* (jogging, cycling, sailing, skating).

Ver la tele – to watch TV

Remember to say *la* tele because in English we just "watch TV".

Ir al colegio en coche – to go to school by car

Al, which literally means "to the" is a combination of *a* and *el*. Sometimes it's logical (*"al* cine" means "*to the* cinema") but we have to remember that we go "to *the* school", not just to school.

Ir al colegio a pie – to go to school on foot

We had "by car" above, but if you are not taking any transport, use "a".

Ir de compras – to go shopping

Escuchar música - to listen to music (the "to" is built in)

Test on using infinitives instead of present tense

1. I'm going to listen to music

2. I want to play football

3. I usually clean the house

4. I have to do my homework

5. I usually watch TV

6. I like doing sport

7. I can go to school on foot

8. Can one buy food?

Answers

1. Voy a escuchar musica

2. Quiero jugar al futbol

3. Suelo limpiar la casa

4. Tengo que hacer mis deberes

5. Suelo ver la tele

6. Me gusta hacer deporte

7. Puedo ir al colegio a pie

8. ¿Se puede comprar comida?

Vocabulary relating to family and descriptions of people

en mi familia	in my family
mi padre	my father
mi madre	my mother
mis padres	my parents
mis hermanos	my siblings
mi hermano	my brother
mi hermana	my sister
mis hermanastros	my step-siblings
mi hermanastro	my half or step-brother
mi hermanastra	my half or step-sister
mayor / menor	older/younger
soy hijo único	I'm an only child *(unique)*
mis abuelos	my grandparents
mi primo / mi prima	my cousin
mi tío	my uncle *(go for tea oh?)*
mi tía	my aunt
gemelos, gemelas	twins
el hijo	son
la hija	daughter
el bebé	baby
el marido	husband *(married-o)*
la mujer / esposa	wife
el chico	boy
la chica	girl
no tengo hermanos	I don't have any siblings
mi hermano se llama	my brother is called

How you get on

nos llevamos bien	we get on well
tenemos mucho en común	we have a lot in common
nos gusta	we like (a singular thing)
nos gustan	we like (plural things)
nos gusta la misma música	we like the same music
nos gustan los mismos programas	we like the same programmes
a veces discutimos	sometimes we argue
estar mimado	to be spoilt
no le gusta(n)	he / she doesn't like
no le gusta mi música	he / she doesn't like my music

Types of family

hay muchos tipos de familia	there are lots of types of family
familias tradicionales	traditional families
familias monoparentales	single-parent families
familias ensambladas	blended families
personas solteras	single people
el número crece	the number is growing
cada vez más	more and more
tienen su valor	they have their value
buenas relaciones	good relations
una relación	a relationship

enamorarse de alguien	to fall in love with someone
el amor	love
conocer a	to meet
se conocen	they meet
se conocen desde hace	they have known each other for
el novio / la novia	boyfriend / girlfriend
casarse con	to marry *(house yourself)*
estar casado /-a	to be married
están casados	they are married
un vínculo	a bond
prometer	to promise
volver a casarse	to remarry
volvió a casarse	he / she remarried
volvieron a casarse	they remarried
una pareja	a couple *(pair)*
embarazada	pregnant
fiel	faithful
leal	loyal
juntos	together *(roads at junction)*
una cita	a date
un beso	a kiss
un abrazo	a hug *(brazo = arm)*
contar con	to rely on *(count on)*
estar divorciado /-a	to be divorced
estar separado /-a	to be separated
estar preocupado	to be worried
discutir	to argue

discutimos sobre	we argue about
llorar	to cry
echar de menos	to miss
la echo de menos	I miss her
lo importante	the important thing
lo único	the only thing

Adjectives to describe people

grande	big
pequeño /-a	small *(like a Pekinese dog)*
alto /-a	tall *(altitude)*
bajo /-a	short *(base)*
simpático /-a	nice *(sympathetic)*
antipático /-a	not nice
alegre	cheerful
triste	sad *(in need of treats!)*
hablador /-a	chatty *(from hablar = to speak)*
trabajador /-a	hardworking *(from trabajar = to work)*
terco /-a	stubborn
delgado /-a	thin *(delicate)*
gordo /-a	fat
interesante	interesting
aburrido /-a	boring
divertido-a	fun *(diverting)*
gracioso/-a	funny *(gracias for being funny)*
serio /-a	serious
valiente	brave *(valiant)*

fuerte	strong *(a fort is strong)*
débil	weak *(a debilitating illness)*
cariñoso /-a	kind
amistoso /-a	friendly *(from amigo)*
tacaño /- a	mean
travieso /-a	naughty
pesado /-a	annoying
guapo /-a	good looking
feo /-a	ugly
viejo /-a	old
joven	young
deportista	sporty
perezoso /-a	lazy
orgulloso /-a	proud

Qualifying your adjectives

siempre	always
a veces	sometimes
de vez en cuando	from time to time
a menudo	often
muy	very
extremadamente	extremely
bastante	quite
un poco	a bit
más / menos…. que yo	more / less … than me

Hair adjectives – "tengo el pelo …"

largo	long
corto	short
liso	straight
rizado	curly
rubio	blonde
marrón	brown
castaño	dark brown
negro	black
pelirrojo	red

General appearance

es calvo	he is bald
es bajo	he is short
es alto	he is tall
lleva gafas	he wears glasses
una barba	a beard *(like barbed wire)*
tiene barba	he has a beard
un bigote	a moustache *('e got a' 'bigote')*
tiene bigote	he has a moustache
me parezco a mi madre	I look like my mother
se parece a su madre	he / she looks like his / her mother
nos parecemos	we look like each other

Clothes and things you carry

una camisa	a shirt *(camisole)*
una camiseta	a t-shirt *(little camisa)*

pantalones	trousers *(pants are long)*
vaqueros	jeans
un vestido	a dress *(long vest)*
una falda	a skirt *('folded' pleats?)*
los guantes	gloves
calcetines	socks *(concertina down legs)*
un cinturón	a belt *(from cintura = waist)*
una corbata	tie *(bat the flies away with it)*
una chaqueta	a jacket
un gorro	woolly hat
gafas	glasses
un paraguas	umbrella *(para agua = for water)*
un jersey	a jumper
zapatos	shoes
zapatillas de deporte	trainers
un abrigo	an overcoat
un impermeable	a raincoat *(impermeable)*
un monedero	wallet *(keep your 'money der')*
una maleta	suitcase *(need a mallet to shut it)*
una bolsa	a bag
un reloj	a watch or clock

Describing clothes

A rayas	striped
a cuadros	checked *(quadrants)*
ajustado /-a	tight *(needs adjusting!)*
con puntitos	spotty *(punto = dot)*

de cuero	leather
de lana	woollen *(from a llama?)*
de seda	silk
de algodón	cotton *(coddon)*
la moda	fashion
la marca	the brand

How much can you remember?

1. How can we avoid conjugating verbs?

2. How do we agree adjectives?

3. How does the verb *hablar* go in the present tense?

4. Name 8 items of clothing in Spanish.

5. What are the four words for *the*?

For your oral and writing

The standard story for describing a person

Use this story to describe any member of your family or any friend or teacher. Don't bother thinking up new hair colours and eye colours – just use the same ones each time. Use any chance you get to do this, even when describing an outing, describe who you went with.

Key to remembering it

Begin with the **name**. Remember that *se llama* means *is called* and *que se llama* means *who is called.*

Now do **three** things that take *tener* (age, hair and eyes)

Now **three** that take *ser* (they are very … but a bit ….. and *more sporty* than me)

Finally, learn my long "**normalmente**" sentence. You won't regret it!

En mi familia hay cuatro personas – mi madre, mi padre, mi hermana y yo. Mi hermana se llama Daisy y tiene quince años. Tiene el pelo rubio y los ojos azules. Es muy inteligente pero un poco tímida y es más deportista que yo. Normalmente nos llevamos bien porque tenemos muchas cosas en común, como el tenis, pero a veces discutimos porque no le gusta mi música.

In my family there are 4 people – my father, my mother, my sister and me. My sister is called Daisy and she is 15. She has blue eyes and blonde hair. She is very intelligent but a bit shy and she is more sporty than me. Normally we get on well because we have lots of things in common like tennis but sometimes we argue because she doesn't like my music.

Other topics

You may be asked about role models. The key here is to use *debería* or *tiene que* to explain what they should or must be or do. When talking about your hobbies, use a variety of structures and give reasons.

Role models Un modelo a seguir debería dar buen ejemplo en todo. Debería ser simpático, comprensivo, inteligente y no tiene que ser perfecto. Los jóvenes deberían respetarse sin compararse a otras personas y hay que seguir modelos que muestran que hay cosas más importantes en la vida.

A role model should give a good example in everything. They should be kind, understanding, intelligent and need not be perfect. Young people need to learn to respect themselves without comparing themselves to others, and one should follow role models who show that there are more important things in life.

Talking / writing about your interests and hobbies

Cuando tengo tiempo / una vez a la semana / todos los días / el sábado, me gusta hacer ciclismo con mi padre y los fines de semana suelo jugar al tenis con mi amigo en el parque porque es mi deporte favorito y soy adicto. Tengo suerte porque soy miembro de un club de tenis desde hace dos años. Paso mucho tiempo viendo la televisión, aunque sea malo para la salud, para relajarme y olvidar el estrés del colegio. Tengo ganas de aprendera jugar al ajedrez porque me parece más interesante que ver la tele.

When I have time / once a week / every day / on Saturdays, I like to go cycling with my father and at the weekends I usually play tennis with my friend in the park because it's my favourite sport and I'm addicted to it. I'm lucky because I have been a member of a tennis club for 2 years. I spend a lot of time watching TV, although it is bad for your health, in order to relax and to forget the stress of school. I'd like to learn chess because it seems more interesting than watching TV.

Day 2

In this session you will be revising:

- Irregular and root-changing verbs in the present tense
- Conjugation and use of *ser* and *estar*
- How to express liking
- Vocabulary relating to your town and your house
- Oral and written answers on town, house and routine

Regular verbs in the present (irregulars on next page)

-ar **hablar** (to speak)	-er **comer** (to eat)	-ir **vivir** (to live)
hablo	como	vivo
hablas	comes	vives
habla	come	vive
hablamos	comemos	vivimos
habláis	coméis	vivís
hablan	comen	viven
Similar verbs: ayudar – to help preparar – prepare escuchar – listen to bailar – to dance cantar – to sing limpiar – to clean trabajar – to work estudiar – to study visitar – to visit esperar – hope/wait buscar – to look for mirar – to look at ganar – to earn, win comprar – to buy pagar – to pay (for) necesitar – to need pintar – to paint dibujar – to draw llegar – to arrive charlar – to chat cocinar – to cook contestar – answer	**Similar verbs:** aprender – to learn beber – to drink comprender - understand deber – to have to esconder – to hide responder – to answer vender – to sell	**Similar verbs:** abolir – to abolish añadir – to add aplaudir – applaud abrir – to open asistir a – to attend confundir – confuse decidir – to decide definir – to define describir – describe descubrir – discover cubrir – to cover discutir – to discuss escribir – to write prohibir – prohibit recibir – to receive unir – to unite

Irregular verbs		
hacer – to do	**poner - to put**	**salir – to go out**
hago	pongo	salgo
haces	pones	sales
hace	pone	sale
hacemos	ponemos	salimos
hacéis	ponéis	salís
hacen	ponen	salen
tener – to have	**venir – to come**	**empezar – to begin**
tengo	vengo	empiezo
tienes	vienes	empiezas
tiene	viene	empieza
tenemos	venimos	empezamos
tenéis	venís	empezáis
tienen	vienen	empiezan
ser – to be	**estar – to be**	**ir – to go**
soy	estoy	voy
eres	estás	vas
es	está	va
somos	estamos	vamos
sois	estáis	vais
son	están	van
poder – be able	**jugar – to play**	**volver – to return**
puedo	juego	vuelvo
puedes	juegas	vuelves
puede	juega	vuelve
podemos	jugamos	volvemos
podéis	jugáis	volvéis
pueden	juegan	vuelven
decir – to say	**dar – to give**	**pensar – to think**
digo	doy	pienso
dices	das	piensas
dice	da	piensa
decimos	damos	pensamos
decís	dais	pensáis
dicen	dan	piensan

Some special uses of irregular verbs

Tener *que*	to have to
Pienso *que*	I think *that* (don't forget *que*)
Dice *que*	he / she says *that* (don't forget *que*)
Es alto (characteristic)	he / she is tall
Está en casa (position)	he / she is at home (in house)
Juego *al* tenis	I play tennis
Hace sol	it's sunny
Hace cinco años	5 years ago
Se puede	one can
Voy *al* cine	I go to the cinema
Vuelvo a casa	I go home (return to house)
Pongo la mesa	I lay the table
Nos dan muchos deberes	They give us a lot of homework

Test on present tense

1. I have to work but I think it's fun.
2. Can I go home now?
3. I play football when it's sunny.
4. We go to the cinema every week.
5. When I go home, I lay the table.
6. I think he's in France.
7. They say that Madrid is interesting.
8. The teachers give us homework.

Answers

1. Tengo que trabajar, pero pienso que es divertido.

2. ¿Puedo volver a casa ahora?

3. Juego al futbol cuando hace sol.

4. Vamos al cine cada semana.

5. Cuando vuelvo a casa, pongo la mesa.

6. Pienso que está en Francia.

7. Dicen que Madrid es interesante.

8. Los profes nos dan deberes.

Ser and *estar* explained

You use *ser* **to describe the characteristics** of a thing or person, and *estar* **to describe states of emotion and position**. Most of the time, *estar* will be used with temporary states, to describe feelings or emotions and where someone or something currently is.

Here are the verbs conjugated in full:

ser (characteristic)	estar (emotion / position)	
soy	estoy	I am
eres	estás	you (s) are
es	está	he, she, it is
somos	estamos	we are
sois	estáis	you are
son	están	they are

Here are some examples of their use:

¿Dónde está el hotel?	Where is the hotel?
¿Tu hermano es simpático?	Is your brother nice?
La casa es muy grande (chara.)	The house is very big
La casa está en Londres (position)	The house is in London
La casa está sucia (currently)	The house is dirty
La cocina está limpia (currently)	The kitchen is clean
El hombre es tímido (chara.)	The man is shy
El hombre está casado ('emotion')	The man is married
Los gatos están contentos (emotion)	The cats are happy

Adjectives that go with *ser*

grande	big
pequeño	small
alto	tall
bajo	short
nuevo	new
antiguo / histórico / viejo	old
guapo	good-looking
joven	young
turístico	touristy
animado	lively
tímido	shy
divertido	fun

aburrido	boring
interesante	interesting
importante	important
inteligente	intelligent
español / inglés	Spanish / English

Adjectives that go with *estar*

casado	married
separado	separated
divorciado	divorced
contento	happy
enfadado	angry
cansado	tired
furioso	furious
estresado	stressed

Positions with *estar*

en casa	at home
en Londres / España	in London / Spain
cerca de	near
lejos de	far from
delante de	in front of
detrás de	behind
al lado de	next to
debajo de	under

An extra use of *estar* – to say what you *are doing*

Spanish allows you to say that you are *in the process of* doing something as well as that you do it. You can say *I'm eating*, as well as *I eat*. This is what we call the present continuous.

Estoy hablando	I am talking
Estás escuchando	you are listening
Está jugando	s/he is playing
Estoy buscando	I'm looking for
Estamos trabajando	we are working
Estáis limpiando	you are cleaning
Están comiendo	they are eating
Estoy bebiendo	I am drinking
Estoy aprendiendo	I am learning
Están viendo la tele	they are watching TV
Estoy limpiando	I am cleaning
Estamos reciclando	we are recycling
Estamos comunicando	we are communicating
Estáis preparando	you (pl) are preparing
Está nadando	s/he is swimming
Está cantando	s/he is singing
Estamos esperando	we are waiting

Test yourself on *ser* and *estar*

1. Estoy esperando
2. Está furiosa
3. Están cansados
4. Están casados
5. Soy alto
6. Son aburridos
7. Está en Madrid
8. Soy deportista
9. Somos divertidos
10. Estamos charlando
11. Están bebiendo vino

Answers

1. I'm waiting
2. She is furious
3. They are tired
4. They are married
5. I am tall
6. They are boring
7. He / she is in Madrid
8. I am sporty
9. We are fun
10. We are chatting
11. They are drinking wine

Liking things

Expressing liking, using the verb *gustar*

Revise this by testing yourself on the examples below:

Me gusta bail**ar**	I like dancing
No me gusta nada limpi**ar**	I don't like cleaning at all
Me gusta el perro	I like the dog
Me gusta**n los perros**	I like dog**s**
No me gusta**n** nada **las manzanas**	I don't like apple**s** at all
Le gusta comer	S/he likes eating
Les gusta bailar	They like dancing
No les gusta**n los** mariscos	They don't like seafood
A mi hermano le gusta beber	My brother likes drinking
A mis padres les gustar comer	My parents like eating
A mi hermana no le gusta el sol	My sister doesn't like the sun
A Fernando no le gusta**n los** gatos	Fernando doesn't like cats

What do you observe here?

- Firstly, the structure is *"to me pleases X"* rather than *"I like X"*.

- Secondly, there is no -ing after the like verb. Use an infinitive instead. *Me gusta nadar* rather than *me gusta nadando*

- Thirdly, when the thing that you like is plural, you add an *n* to the liking verb. Where there's an *s* there's an *n*...

- To add a complication, if someone else likes something, we have to change the pronoun *me* to *te, le, nos, os,* or *les*.

Me gusta(n) *add n if the thing you like is plural* I like

Te gusta(n)   you (s) like

Le gusta(n)   he/she likes

Nos gusta(n)   we like

Os gusta(n)   you (pl) like

Les gusta(n)   they like

- If we are naming the person who likes the thing, then add *a*

  A Fred le gusta bailar   Fred likes dancing

Test yourself on *gustar*

1. I like dogs

2. I like the dog

3. I like chocolate

4. He likes pizza

5. They like the house

Answers

1. Me gustan los perros

2. Me gusta el perro

3. Me gusta el chocolate

4. Le gusta la pizza

5. Les gusta la casa

Vocabulary

Describing where you live

el país	country
la región	region
el barrio	neighbourhood
la ciudad	city / town
el pueblo	village
en el campo	in the countryside
la mejor región de…	the best region of
en mi barrio	in my area *(barriers protect)*
en la ciudad	in the city *(-dad ending = ity)*
en mi pueblo	in my village
mucho que hacer	a lot to do
vivo aquí desde hace…	I have lived here for…
las ventajas	advantages

Places in the town

hay	there is / are
un lugar / un sitio	place *(lug your stuff there)*
donde se puede	where you can
un cine	cinema
restaurantes	restaurants
polideportivos	sports centres
colegios	schools
un centro comercial	a shopping centre
mercados	markets

supermercados	supermarkets
iglesias	churches
parques	parks
almacenes	department stores
tiendas	shops
fábricas	factories
una playa	a beach
una piscina	a pool
la acera	the pavement
la zona peatonal	the pedestrian zone
la red de transporte	the transport network

Things to do in town

visitar	to visit
museos	museums
un palacio	palace
un castillo	castle
una galería	gallery
un monumento	monument
sitios turísticos	tourist attractions
sitios históricos	historical sites
restaurantes	restaurants
ir al restaurante	to go to a restaurant
comer	to eat
teatros	theatres
ir al teatro	to go to the theatre

ver un espectáculo	to see a show
una obra de teatro	a play
cines	cinemas
ir al cine	to go to the cinema
ver una película	to see a film
ir a la pista de hielo	to go to the ice rink
hacer patinaje	to go skating
ir a la piscina	to go to the pool
hacer natación	to go swimming
nadar	to swim
ir de compras	to go shopping
hacer deporte	to do sport
ir a la bolera	to go bowling
salir por la noche	to go out at night
salir a bailar	to go out dancing
salir a comer	to go out to eat
pasear al perro	to walk the dog
dar paseos	to go for walks
dar una vuelta en bici	to go for a bike ride
montar en bici	to cycle
hacer ciclismo	to cycle
descansar	to rest / relax
encontrarse con amigos	to meet up with friends
tomar una copa	to have a drink
estudiar	to study

Past and future living

cuando era joven	when I was young
vivía en el campo	I lived in the countryside
había menos tiendas	there were fewer shops
era menos ruidoso	it was less noisy
cuando sea mayor	when I'm older
voy a seguir viviendo aquí	I'm going to carry on living here
para que pueda	so that I can
aprovechar	to make the most of

Town positives

lo bueno es que	the good thing is that
lo que más me gusta es	what I like most is
paso mucho tiempo	I spend lots of time
suelo pasar tiempo	I usually spend time
recomendaría	I would recommend
se puede	one can
no hay que…	it isn't necessary to…
no tienes que…	you don't have to…

Town negatives and improvements

lo malo es que	the bad thing is that
lo que falta es	what's missing is
lo que no me gusta es	what I don't like is
no hay	there isn't a… / there aren't any…
hay que	it is necessary to

tienes que	you have to
no se puede	one can't
desventajas	disadvantages
atascos	traffic jams *('a task' getting through)*
el tráfico	traffic
la contaminación	pollution
los coches producen	the cars produce
gases de escape	exhaust fumes
el ruido	the noise *(ruins it all)*
tirar basura	to drop litter
la gente tira basura	people drop litter
caro	expensive *(expensive car)*
la calle	the street
lleno	full
sucio	dirty
concurrido	busy, crowded
si pudiera	if I could
cambiaría	I'd change
construiría	I'd build
mejoraría	I'd improve
me gustaría tener	I'd like to have
aunque sea	although it is
no me gusta(n)	I don't like
me preocupa	it worries me
me fastidia	it annoys me

Shopping

ir de compras	to go shopping
ir a comprar	to go shopping
hacer la(s) compra(s)	to go shopping (for provisions)
comprar	to buy
devolver	to return
ir al centro comercial	to go to the shopping centre
abierto	open *(open 'a-beer-too'!)*
cerrado	closed
dinero	money *('dinner' money)*
el descuento	discount
las rebajas	the sales
hacer cola	to queue *(for coca 'cola')*
gastar	to spend *(on 'gas' bill)*
malgastar	to waste *(bad spend)*
demasiado grande	too big
demasiado pequeño	too small
ahorrar	to save
baratas / rebajas	sales
el / la dependiente	shop assistant
probarse	to try on
una tarjeta de crédito	a credit card
no puedo permitírmelo	I can't afford it
mirar escaparates	to go window-shopping
comprar en linea	to buy online

Countryside

mudarse	to move house
en el campo	in the countryside
hay menos ruido	there is less noise
es menos concurrido	it's less crowded
tranquilo	quiet
bonito	pretty
el paisaje	the scenery
vacío	empty *(vacant)*
espacios verdes	green spaces
aislado	isolated
difícil desplazarse	difficult to get about
al aire libre	in the fresh air

Houses and flats

una casa	a house
independiente	detached
unifamiliar	semi-detached
adosada	terraced
un piso / un apartamento	a flat
en la planta baja	on the ground floor
en el primer piso	on the first floor
en el segundo piso	on the second floor
la puerta principal	the front door
la puerta trasera	the back door

Rooms

la habitación	room *(you inhabit it)*
el dormitorio	bedroom *(dormitory)*
la cocina	kitchen *('cook-in-a' kitchen)*
el jardín	garden
el salón	lounge *(saloon)*
el garaje	garage
el vestíbulo	hall
el descansillo	landing
el comedor	dining room *(from comer=to eat)*
el despacho	office *(send your dispatches)*
la terraza interior	conservatory *(interior terrace)*
el balcón	balcony
un lavadero	utility room
una sala de juegos	games room

Structure

el edificio	building *(Eddy fixed it)*
la ventana	window *(for ventilation)*
la puerta	door *(port is a door to a country)*
las paredes	walls *(a pair of Eddy's)*
el tejado	roof
el techo	ceiling
la escalera	staircase *(escalator)*
la calefacción central	central heating

Furniture

los muebles	furniture
el armario	wardrobe *(for your 'armour')*
la cómoda	chest of drawers
la alfombra	rug
la cama	bed
la almohada	pillow
la estantería	bookshelf *('it stand here')*
el lavaplatos	dishwasher
la lavadora	washing machine
el grifo	tap *(grip it)*
el espejo	mirror *(looking 'especially' lovely)*
el horno	oven
el césped	lawn
el árbol	tree
la hierba	grass *(green herbs)*
las flores	flowers
detrás de	behind *(leave trash behind)*
delante de	in front of *(you leant on it)*
al lado de	next to *('a lad' next to you)*
cerca de	near
compartir	to share *(into compartments)*
limpio	clean *(limp after all the cleaning)*
sucio	dirty
desordenado	untidy
los vecinos	neighbours *('they've seen us!')*

Household jobs

suelo	I usually
suelo pasar la aspiradora	I usually do the hoovering
poner la mesa	to lay the table
quitar la mesa	to clear the table
lavar los platos	to wash the dishes
preparar la comida	to do the cooking
arreglar mi dormitorio	to tidy my room
ayudar a mis padres	to help my parents
lavar el coche	to wash the car
limpiar la cocina	to clean the kitchen
hacer jardinería	to do the gardening
sacar la basura	to take out the rubbish *(in a sack)*
hacer de canguro	to do babysitting *(with baby in pouch)*
llenar el lavaplatos	to fill the dishwasher

Daily routine

Me levanto	I get up
Me ducho	I shower
Me visto	I get dressed
Desayuno	I have breakfast
Tomo un café	I have a coffee
Voy al colegio	I go to school
Llego al colegio	I arrive at school
Juego con mis amigos	I play with my friends
Voy a mis clases	I go to my lessons

Vuelvo a casa	I go home
Hago mis deberes	I do my homework
Ceno	I have dinner
Veo la tele	I watch TV
Me acuesto	I go to bed

How much can you remember?

1. How does the verb *gustar* work?

2. Give examples of *gustar* in its different forms

3. Use *jugar* in a sentence

4. What does *se puede* mean?

5. What's the difference between *ser* and *estar*?

6. How do you express the continuous present in Spanish?

For your oral and writing

Standard story for describing a place

Use the story below to describe your town or your house (or your school). Look at how we are just changing a few words and phrases here and there but keeping the structure the same. You can watch me do this on my YouTube channel Lucy Martin Tuition.

Key to remembering it: Begin with the name or place. Then three adjectives to describe it. Then what I call the 4-point sentence, because the words in bold show you where the level 9 points are. Then say what you like, what you don't like, and how you'd improve it. When asked about what there is for young people / tourists in your town, what's wrong with it, what you'd change, why you like it etc, you can just pick out the right bits of the speech.

Describing your town (also house, school, anything!)

Mi barrio se llama Wimbledon. Es grande, moderno y agradable. **Tengo suerte** porque **en mi opinión** es la **mejor** región de Londres y vivo allí **desde hace** cinco años.

Lo que más me gusta es que hay un montón de cosas que hacer. Hay un cine donde se pueden ver películas y un parque donde suelo pasar mucho tiempo haciendo deporte.

Lo malo es que hay mucha contaminación. Si pudiera cambiar algo habría menos tráfico.

My town is called Wimbledon. It's big, modern and nice. I'm lucky because in my opinion it's the best region of London and I've been living there 5 years. What I like is that there are lots of things to do – a cinema where you can watch films and a park where I usually spend a lot of time doing sport. The bad thing is that there is a lot of pollution. If I could change something there would be less traffic.

Describing your house (same pattern)

Mi casa está en Wimbledon. Es grande, moderna y agradable. Tengo suerte porque en mi opinión es la mejor casa de mi barrio y vivo allí desde hace cinco años. Lo que más me gusta es que hay un montón de cosas que hacer – un salón donde se puede ver la tele y un jardín donde suelo pasar mucho tiempo jugando al futbol. Lo malo es que mi dormitorio es demasiado pequeño. Si fuera más grande estaría contenta.

My house is in Wimbledon. It's big, modern and nice. I'm lucky because in my opinion it's the best house in my neighbourhood and I've been living there 5 years. What I like is that there are lots of things to do (or everything I need) – a sitting room where you can watch TV and a garden where you can play football. What I don't like is that my room is too small. If it was bigger, I would be happy.

Describing your school (same pattern)

Mi colegio se llama Brookfield High School y está en Wimbledon cerca de Londres. Tengo suerte porque en mi opinión es el mejor colegio del mundo y voy allí desde hace cinco años. Lo que más me gusta es que hay un montón de cosas que hacer. Hay un campo deportivo donde se puede jugar al futbol, y una biblioteca donde suelo pasar muchas horas trabajando, pero lo malo es que no hay piscina. Si hubiera una piscina, sería perfecto.

My school is called Brookfield High school and it is in Wimbledon near London. I'm lucky because in my opinion it's the best school in the world and I've been going there for 5 years. What I like most is that there are loads of things to do. There is a sports field where you can play football and a library where I usually spend many hours working, but the bad thing is that there isn't a pool. If there was a pool it would be perfect.

Daily routine

Normalmente, por la mañana me pego un madrugón porque tengo que ir al colegio. Me despierto a las siete, me levanto, me ducho y me visto antes de desayunar. Voy al colegio en autobús a las ocho y al llegar, charlo con mis amigos. Las clases empiezan a las nueve y tenemos ocho clases de cuarenta minutos al día. Vuelvo a casa a las cuatro y media, hago mis deberes, ceno con mi familia y después de cenar, suelo ver la tele en el salón o chatear por internet con mis amigos. Me acuesto sobre las diez.

Normally in the morning I have to get up really early because I have to go to school. I wake up at 7, I get up, shower and get dressed before having breakfast. I go to school by bus at 8 and when I arrive I chat to my friends. Lessons begin at 9 and we have 8 lessons of 40 minutes each per day. I go home at 4.30, do my homework, eat with my family and after eating I usually watch TV in the lounge or chat online with my friends. I go to bed around 10.

Weekend routine

El fin de semana, suelo levantarme más tarde que normalmente porque no tengo que ir al colegio. Desayuno sobre las once y salgo con mis amigos al parque o al centro comercial para ir de compras. Por la tarde suelo jugar al tenis en el polideportivo, y siempre cenamos juntos en familia. A veces vemos una película en Netflix o pasamos la tarde jugando a las cartas. Paso unas horas haciendo mis deberes, pero suelo dejarlos para el final.

At the weekend I get up later than usual because I don't have to go to school. I have breakfast around 11 and I go out with my friends to the park or the shopping centre to go shopping. In the afternoon I usually play tennis at the sports centre, and we always have dinner together as a family. Sometimes we watch a film on Netflix or we spend the evening playing cards. I spend a few hours doing my homework, but I usually leave it until the last minute.

Transport in your region

Hay trenes, autobuses y el metro y los billetes son baratos. Lo único es que las calles son ruidosas y hay demasiados atascos. Si hubiera más rutas para ciclistas pienso que no habría tanta contaminación del aire.

There are trains, buses and the underground and the tickets are cheap. The only thing is that the streets are noisy and there are too many traffic jams. If there were more cycle paths, I think there wouldn't be so much air pollution.

Helping at home

Para ayudar mis padres lavo los platos / el coche, arreglo mi dormitorio, paso la aspiradora, pongo / quito la mesa, preparo la comida y a veces limpio la cocina. No obstante, me cuesta hacerlo ahora porque los profes nos dan tantos deberes y paso mucho tiempo revisando para mis exámenes. Si tuviera menos deberes, haría más para ayudar.

To help my parents I wash the dishes / the car, I tidy my room, I hoover, I lay / clear the table, I cook meals and sometimes I clean the kitchen. However, I struggle to do it now because the teachers give us so much homework and I spend a lot of time revising for exams. If I had less homework I would do more to help.

Cooking at home

Por lo general, mi madre prepara la comida, pero cuando no está, lo hago yo. Me gusta cocinar, y si tuviera tiempo haría más, pero los profes nos dan demasiados deberes.

In general, my mother cooks the meals, but when she's not there, I do it. I like cooking, and if I had the time I would do more, but the teachers give us too much homework.

Your bedroom

Está en el primer piso al lado del dormitorio de mis padres.

Al lado de la cama hay un armario y delante de la ventana hay un escritorio donde hago mis deberes. Las paredes son azules porque es mi color favorito, y tengo suerte porque tengo no solo un ordenador portátil sino también una televisión, así que puedo fácilmente pasar muchísimas horas relajándome sin tener que bajar la escalera.

My bedroom is on the first floor by my parents' bedroom. Next to the bed there is a cupboard and in front of the window is a desk where I do my homework. The walls are blue because it's my favourite colour and I'm lucky because I not only have a laptop but also a television so I can easily spend many hours relaxing without having to go downstairs.

Pocket money and shopping

Tengo suerte porque mis padres me dan treinta euros al mes. Normalmente suelo comprar revistas y caramelos, pero el fin de semana pasado lo gasté en ir al cine con mis amigos. Si tuviera la oportunidad, me gustaría tener más dinero para que pudiera comprar más videojuegos, pero mis padres creen que tengo suficiente dinero. ¡Qué pesadilla! No creo que tengan razón.

I am lucky because my parents give me thirty euros a month. Normally, I buy magazines or videogames, but last weekend I spent it on going to the cinema with my friends. If I had the chance, I would like more money so that I can buy more sweets but my parents think that I get enough money. What a nightmare! I don't think they are right.

NOTES

Day 3

In this session you will be revising:

- Direct object pronouns
- Using reflexive verbs
- The personal *a*
- Vocabulary relating to health
- Oral and written answers on health

Pronouns

Using pronouns as direct objects (*eg. I see him / she sees me*)

The main pronouns are *lo*, *la* (it) and *los*, *las* (them) but you will also need to be able to say *me, him, us, them, you* etc

Look at the verb *ver* = to see

veo	I see
ves	you (s) see
ve	he / she / it sees
vemos	we see
veis	you (pl) see
ven	they see

We can put personal pronouns in front of verbs (where in English they come after the verb)

he sees me	me ve (the "me" comes first)
lo veo	I see him (or it, with a masculine noun)
la veo	I see her (or it, with a feminine noun)
los veo	I see them (masculine)
las veo	I see them (feminine)
nos ven	they see us
nos ve	he / she sees us

Test yourself on pronouns

Lo vemos	We see him (or it, with a masculine noun)
La vemos	We see her (or it, with a feminine noun)
Los vemos	We see them (masculine)

Las vemos	We see them (feminine)
La como	I eat it (eg. la pizza)
Los como	I eat them (eg. los caramelos)
Las como	I eat them (eg. las fresas)
La bebo	I drink it (eg. la cerveza)
Las conozco	I know them (eg. las chicas)

Pronouns on the end of verbs

After an infinitive, or a gerund (which is the *-ando -iendo* ending), you can actually stick the pronoun on the end.

No me gusta beberlo	I don't like drinking it
Quiero comerlos	I want to eat them
Suelen ayudarnos	They usually help us
Voy a verla	I'm going to see her
Van a comprarlas	They are going to buy them
Va a ayudarme	He / she is going to help me.
Estoy comiendolo	I'm eating it
Van a ayudarme	They are going to help me
Estoy bcbiéndolo	I'm drinking it
Vamos a comprarlo	We are going to buy it
No me gusta comerlos	I don't like eating them
Estoy haciéndolos	I'm doing it (homework!)
Estoy comiéndolos	I am eating them
Vamos a hacerlo	We are going to do it
Le gusta verlos	She likes watching them

Reflexive verbs

These exist to express things that you do to *yourself* ie. shower, wash, brush teeth, wake up and get up. You can shower (duchar) someone else, or you can shower yourself (duchar**se**). You can wash something or someone else (lavar) or wash yourself (lavar**se**). You can lift up something (levantar) or get yourself up out of bed (levantar**se**). If you want to use these verbs in the *I* form, in any tense just put *me* on the front (pronounced *"meh"* not *"me"*).

Me levanto	from levantarse	I get up
Me ducho	from ducharse	I shower
Me lavo	from lavarse	I wash (myself)
Me acuesto	from acostarse	I go to bed
Me visto	from vestirse	I get dressed
Me divierto	from divertirse	I have fun
Me quedo	from quedarse	I stay
Me relajo	from relajarse	I relax

Here's how it goes when it's other people doing it:

Me levanto	I get up
Te levantas	you get up
Se levanta	he / she gets up
Nos levantamos	we get up
Os levantáis	you (pl) get up
Se levantan	they get up

Example

Por la manana, me levanto, me ducho y me visto. Normalmente durante el día me quedo en casa, me relajo y me divierto. Me acuesto temprano porque estoy siempre cansado.

In the morning, I get up, I have a shower and I get dressed. During the day, I normally stay at home, relax and have fun. I go to bed early because I am always tired.

The personal *a*

If I say "I see the boy*", the boy* is the direct object of the verb *to see*. Similarly with "I help my friend", the *friend* is the direct object of the verb *to help*.

In Spanish, where the direct object of a verb is animate (ie. alive) then it must be preceded by the word "*a*", which normally means "*to*" but in this case is just recognition of the next noun being a living thing. You might imagine this to be putting some polite distance between you and the other person, but bear in mind that it might be an animal too. If it is a masculine singular noun, you will need to condense the "*a*" and the "*el*" to form "*al*", so you can't say *veo a el perro*, you say *veo al perro*. Here are some verbs that might need the *a*.

ayudar	to help
mirar	to look at
pasear	to walk (eg. dog)
odiar	to hate
animar	to encourage
escuchar	to listen to
acompañar	to accompany
conocer	to know (a person)
buscar	to look for

Don't use the personal a with tener (*tengo un hermano* NOT *a un hermano*) or with non-specific things (*busco un marido* NOT *a un marido*).

Test yourself

Busco un marido	I'm looking for a husband
Busco a mi madre	I'm looking for my mother
Veo a mucha gente	I can see lots of people
Conoci a gente nueva	I met new people
Ayudo a mis padres	I help my parents
Escucho al profe	I listen to the teacher
Me gusta pasear al perro	I like walking the dog
Estoy mirando al chico	I'm looking at the boy

El gobierno debería animar a la gente a reciclar
The government should encourage people to recycle

Vocabulary

Healthy lifestyle

la salud	health
malo para la salud	bad for your health
bueno para la salud	good for your health
sano / saludable	healthy
unos consejos	some advice
llevar una vida sana	to lead a healthy life
una dieta sana	a healthy diet
una dieta equilibrada	a balanced diet
la cantidad	quantity *(dad= ity)*
cinco porciones de	5 portions of
fruta y verduras	fruit and vegetables
deberíamos	we should
intentar	to try to
comer sano	eat healthily
evitar	avoid
la comida basura	junk food
el azúcar	sugar
la materia grasa	fat *(greasy)*
el alcohol	alcohol
tomar drogas	to take drugs
fumar	to smoke
hacer ejercicio	to do exercise
hacer deporte	to do sport
al aire libre	in the fresh air

dormir	to sleep
puede causar	it can cause
enfermedades graves	serious illnesses
el cáncer	cancer
la obesidad	obesity
se puede	you can
enfermarse	to get sick
engordar	to get fat
aunque sea malo	although it's bad
para la salud	for your health
el ocio	leisure
en mi tiempo libre	in my free time
hago deporte	I do sport
juego al tenis	I play tennis
me gusta hacer	I like doing
me gusta jugar	I like playing

Sports that take *hacer*

deporte	sport
natación	swimming
equitación	horseriding
windsurf	windsurfing
vela	sailing *(turn the v over - sail)*
patinaje	skating *(pat the ice)*
gimnasia	gymnastics
ciclismo	cycling

piragüismo	canoeing
alpinismo	mountaineering
atletismo	athletics

Playing ball-games

jugar al baloncesto	to play basketball
jugar al fútbol	to play football
jugar al hockey	to play hockey
jugar al cricket	to play cricket
un partido de fútbol	a football match
asistir a un partido	to attend a match

People in sport

el jugador	player
el / la futbolista	footballer
el / la tenista	tennis player
el / la ciclista	cyclist
el / la atleta	athlete
el / la torero /-a / matador	bullfighter
el / la campeón /-a	champion
los espectadores	spectators

Sports events

entrenarse	to train
recibir premios	to win prizes
el partido	match

el torneo	tournament
la copa del mundo	the world cup
el campeonato	championship
la carrera	race
en equipo	in a team
el equipo escolar	the school team

Other hobbies

leer periódicos	to read newspapers
leer libros	to read books
leer revistas	to read magazines *(reviews)*
novelas	novels
tebeos	comics
la lectura	reading
dibujar	to draw
pintar	to paint
dar paseos	to go for walks
ir de compras	to go shopping
escuchar música	to listen to music
ver la tele	to watch TV
tocar el piano	to play piano *(toc toc toc)*
tocar la guitarra	to play guitar
cantar	to sing *(chant)*
bailar	to dance *(ballet)*
coleccionar	to collect
pescar	to fish

chatear en línea	to chat online
compartir fotos	to share photos

Cinema and TV

ir al cine	to go to the cinema
ver la tele	to watch TV
una película	a film *(about pelicans?)*
mi película favorita	my favourite film
mi programa favorito	my favourite programme
el canal	channel
telenovelas	soaps
telebasura	rubbish TV
documentales	documentaries
las noticias	the news *(notices)*
educativa	educational
una herramienta útil	a useful tool *(hairy-men tools)*
acabo de ver	I have just seen
una película de horror	horror film
una película de ciencia ficción	sci fi film
una película de guerra	war film
una película policíaca	detective film
una película del oeste	western
una película de amor	romantic film
una película de aventuras	adventure film
dibujos animados	cartoons
trata de	it's about

efectos especiales special effects

Illness

hay el riesgo de	there is the risk of
una enfermedad	an illness
estar mal	to be unwell
sentirse	to feel
toser	to cough
la tos	cough
vomitar	to vomit
estar constipado	to have a cold
un resfriado	a cold
el sida	AIDS
el dolor	pain
una picadura	a bite / sting
la gripe	flu
ir al médico	to go to the doctor
pastillas	pills
medicina	medicine
medicamentos	medicine

Accidents

un accidente	an accident
tuve un accidente	I had an accident
tuvo un accidente	he had an accident
me rompí la pierna	I broke my leg

el incendio	a fire
apagar el incendio	to put out a fire
el humo	smoke
la inundación	flooding
el peligro	danger
un pinchazo	a puncture
tuve un pinchazo	I had a puncture
el riesgo	risk
sangre	blood
una multa	a fine
ayudar	to help
salvar	to save
gritar	to shout
chocar / pegar / golpear	to hit
atropellar	to run over
ocurrir / suceder	to happen
ahogarse	to drown
el herido	the injured person
en la cárcel	in prison

Body parts

el brazo	arm
la mano	hand *(the main thing you need)*
el dedo	finger
el pie	foot
la pierna	leg *(longer than el pie)*

la rodilla	knee
la espalda	back
la cara	face
la oreja / el oído	ear
la cabeza	head *(cabbage)*
la nariz	nose
el estómago	stomach
el pelo	hair
el diente / la muela	tooth
la voz	voice
los ojos	eyes
los hombros	shoulders *(hombres - men)*
la boca	mouth *(for your bocadillo = sandwich)*

How much can you remember?

1. What are the four main object pronouns and where do they go?

2. What is the personal *a*?

3. How do you say *I get up and have a shower*?

4. Name as many body parts as you can

For your oral and writing

What do you eat on a normal day?

Cada mañana desayuno cereales porque son una fuente de energía. Como un bocadillo y fruta en el colegio, pero si tuviera la oportunidad me gustaría comer pescado frito con patatas fritas. Al volver a casa, siempre como chocolate, aunque sea malo para la salud, porque soy adicta y se me hace la boca agua. Ceno carne y verduras, pasta, pollo o pizza. Debería comer menos chocolate y más fruta y verduras para evitar enfermedades cardíacas.

Every morning I eat cereal because it is a source of energy. I eat a sandwich and fruit at school but if I had the chance I would like to eat fish and chips. On returning home, I always eat chocolate although it is bad for you, because I am addicted and it makes my mouth water. I eat meat and vegetables, pasta, chicken or pizza for dinner. I should eat less chocolate and more fruit and vegetables in order to avoid heart problems.

Lunch at school

Suelo almorzar en la cantina donde suelo tomar un bocadillo de pollo o una ensalada. Afortunadamente la comida escolar ha mejorado a lo largo de los años, tanto en cuanto a sabor como a nutrición. ¡Qué suerte tenemos! Ayer comí pasta con champiñones. Fue delicioso.

I eat lunch in the canteen where I usually have a chicken sandwich or a salad. Fortunately, school lunches have improved over the years, in flavour as in nutrition. How lucky we are! Yesterday I ate pasta with mushrooms. It was delicious.

Favourite food

Mi comida favorita es el chocolate, aunque sea malo para la salud, porque es delicioso y se me hace la boca agua. Como chocolate todos los días, después del colegio para que tenga la energía que necesito para hacer mis deberes.

My favourite food is chocolate although it is bad for my health because it is delicious and makes my mouth water. I eat chocolate every day after school so that I have the energy I need to do my homework.

How to stay healthy

Para llevar una vida sana se debe comer una dieta variada con cinco porciones de fruta o verduras al día, ya que nos dan vitaminas importantes. Deberíamos evitar la comida basura porque contiene demasiado azúcar y grasa y provoca obesidad. Además, es muy importante que hagamos deporte, evitemos el alcohol y no fumemos, porque puede causar enfermedades graves. Sin embargo, opino que podemos tomar los alimentos no saludables en moderación.

In order to lead a healthy life, we must eat a varied diet with five portions of fruit and vegetables a day because they give us important vitamins. We should avoid junk food because it contains too much sugar and fat and causes obesity. In addition, it's very important to do sport, avoid alcohol and not smoke because it can cause serious illnesses. However, I think that we can eat unhealthy food in moderation.

How you keep fit

Para mantenerme en forma hago deporte por lo menos tres veces a la semana al aire libre, bebo dos litros de agua al día y tomo cinco porciones de fruta o verduras. Nunca fumo y nunca he probado una droga. Siempre intento evitar la comida basura y materia grasa, aunque sea difícil porque no puedo prescindir del chocolate, e intento dormir ocho horas como mínimo cada noche.

In order to keep in shape, I do sport at least three times a week in the fresh air, I drink two litres of water a day and I have 5 portions of fruit or vegetables. I never smoke and I have never taken drugs. I always try to avoid junk and fatty foods, although it is difficult because I can't manage without chocolate, and I try to sleep eight hours minimum every night.

Do you like sport?

Sí, me gusta muchísimo el deporte. Es mi asignatura favorita en el colegio porque es fácil y el profesor es divertido. Lo que más me gusta es estar al aire libre. Después de una hora de tenis me siento muy relajado. Suelo jugar al tenis tres veces a la semana, y los sábados me encanta aprovechar el buen tiempo y hacer ciclismo con mi padre. Cuando sea mayor, voy a seguir haciendo deporte para mantenerme en forma y un buen estado de ánimo.

Yes, I like sport a lot. It is my favourite subject at school because it is easy and the teacher is fun. What I like the most is being in the fresh air. After an hour of tennis I feel very relaxed. I usually play tennis three times a week and on Saturdays I love to make the most of the good weather and go cycling with my father. When I grow up I'm going to carry on doing sport to keep fit and stay happy.

Why should we do sport?

Deberíamos hacer deporte ya que es genial para mejorar el estado de ánimo, reducir el estrés y mantenerse en forma. Puedes también hacer nuevos amigos y aumentar la autoconfianza. Si no hiciéramos deporte, correríamos el riesgo de engordar, y la obesidad puede provocar enfermedades graves.

We should do sport because it is a great way to improve your mood, reduce stress and keep fit. You can also make new friends and improve your self-confidence. If we didn't do sport, we would risk getting fat and obesity can cause serious illnesses.

Today's health problems

Hay un montón de problemas de salud en mi país, pero lo que más me preocupa es la obesidad. Se dice que casi la mitad de los niños británicos son obesos. Pasan demasiado tiempo delante de la televisión o pegados a sus móviles y no hacen ejercicio. También suelen comer la comida basura porque es barata, sabrosa y fácil a obtener. Contiene mucha grasa, sal y azúcar y eso puede provocar enfermedades como la cardiopatía.

There are loads of health problems in my country. What worries me most is obesity. It is said that almost half of British children are obese. They spend too much time in front of the television or glued to their mobiles and don't exercise. Also they eat junk food because it is cheap, tasty and easy to get. It contains lots of fat, salt and sugar and this can cause illnesses like heart disease.

The solution to health problems

Es imprescindible que hagamos algo para mejorar la situación. Si fuera ministro de deporte, lanzaría una campaña para enseñar a los niños sobre los beneficios del deporte. Sería genial si hubiera unas personas famosas a las que los jóvenes admiran que podrían motivarles a cambiar su estilo de vida. También, es esencial que haya polideportivos en todos partes para que los jóvenes puedan acceder al deporte fácilmente. Ya existen, pero tienes que ser miembro y es caro, así que los jóvenes no pueden permitírselo. Además, la comida sana debería ser más barata.

It is necessary that we do something to improve the situation. If I were minister of sport I would launch a campaign to teach children about the benefits of sport. It would be great if there were some celebrities who young people admired that could motivate them to change their lifestyle. Also, it is essential that there are sports centres everywhere so that young people can access sport easily. They already exist but you have to be a member and it is expensive, therefore young people can't afford it. In addition, healthy food should be cheaper.

Sickness

Tengo suerte porque casi nunca estoy enferma. Normalmente si no es serio, hay que guardar cama, pero si no se sientes mejor después de algunos días, tienes que ir al médico. Evitamos enfermedades llevando un estilo de vida sano.

I am lucky because I am almost never sick. Normally, if it is not serious you have to stay in bed but if you do not feel better after a few days, you have to go to the doctor. We avoid illnesses by living a healthy lifestyle.

Smoking (adapt for alcohol and drugs)

A mi parecer, fumar es absurdo porque todo el mundo sabe que causa enfermedades graves como el cáncer y la bronquitis crónica. Nunca fumaré. Pienso que los jóvenes de hoy en día fuman por un montón de razones, pero lo más importante es la presión del grupo. Si vas a una fiesta y hay muchas personas que están fumando, hay la tentación de hacer lo mismo para sentirse parte del grupo.

In my opinion, smoking is ridiculous because everyone knows that it causes serious illnesses like cancer and chronic bronchitis. I will never smoke. I think that young people today smoke for loads of reasons, but the most important is peer pressure. If you go to a party and there are lots of people smoking, there is the temptation to do the same to feel part of the group.

Vegetarianism

Hay un montón de razones para ser vegetariano. No solo es que no quieren matar a los animales sino también tienen razones relacionadas con la salud y el medioambiente. Algunos dicen que comer carne en exceso es malo para la salud y además la producción de carne destruye las selvas tropicales y el medioambiente.

There are many reasons why people are vegetarian. Not only do they not want to kill animals but also they have reasons to do with health and the environment. Some say that eating excessive amounts of meat is bad for your health and in addition the production of meat destroys tropical forests and the environment.

NOTES

Day 4

In this session you will be revising:

- The preterite tense *(I ate)*
- The perfect tense *(I have eaten)*
- Vocabulary relating to food and holidays
- Oral and written answers on past events

The preterite (past) tense

Hablar (to speak)	Comer (to eat)	Vivir (to live)
hablé	comí	viví
hablaste	comiste	viviste
habló	comió	vivió
hablamos	comimos	vivimos
hablasteis	comisteis	vivisteis
hablaron	comieron	vivieron
hacer – to do	**poner - to put**	**poder – to be able**
hice	puse	pude
hiciste	pusiste	pudiste
hizo	puso	pudo
hicimos	pusimos	pudimos
hicistéis	pusistéis	pudisteis
hicieron	pusieron	pudieron
tener – to have	**venir – to come**	**dar – to give**
tuve	vine	di
tuviste	viniste	diste
tuvo	vino	dio
tuvimos	vinimos	dimos
tuvisteis	vinisteis	disteis
tuvieron	vinieron	dieron
ser / ir –to be / go	**estar – to be**	**decir – to say**
fui	estuve	dije
fuiste	estuviste	dijiste
fue	estuvo	dijo
fuimos	estuvimos	dijimos
fuisteis	estuvisteis	dijisteis
fueron	estuvieron	dijeron

Test yourself on the preterite

Hablé francés durante dos horas	I spoke French for two hours
Hablaron sin parar	They spoke without stopping
¿Hablaste con tus padres?	Did you speak to your parents?
Ayudé a mis padres	I helped my parents
Reciclé el vidrio	I recycled the glass
Trabajamos en equipo	We worked in a team
¿Estudiaste español?	Did you study Spanish?
Comí carne con verduras	I ate meat and vegetables
Tuvieron un accidente	They had an accident
Tuve suerte	I was lucky
Tuvo que volver a casa	He had to go home
Fui a Madrid en avión	I went to Madrid by plane
Fuimos de vacaciones	We went on holiday
Tuvimos éxito	We were successful
Fueron al trabajo	They went to work
Hice mis deberes	I did my homework
Hizo sol	It was sunny
Hicieron ciclismo	They went cycling
Hizo deporte	S/he did sport
Mis abuelos vinieron	My grandparents came
Me dijeron la verdad	They told me the truth
No dijo nada	He didn't say anything

The perfect tense

The structure of the perfect tense, equivalent to the English "I have eaten" is made up of a person ("I"), an auxiliary ("have") and a past participle ("eaten"). The auxiliary ("have") is not the verb *tener*, but another verb (*haber*) used specifically to make this tense. The past participle is made by removing the *ar/er/ir* and adding *-ado* or *-ido* to the verb. You will see that *-ar* verbs go to *-ado* and that *-er* and *-ir* verbs both go the same way - *ido*.

Hablar (to speak)	**Comer** (to eat)	**Vivir** (to live)
he hablado	he comido	he vivido
has hablado	has comido	has vivido
ha hablado	ha comido	ha vivido
hemos hablado	hemos comido	hemos vivido
habéis hablado	habéis comido	habéis vivido
han hablado	han comido	han vivido

Irregular past participles include:

hacer – hecho	ver – visto	volver - vuelto
decir – dicho	abrir – abierto	escribir – escrito
morir – muerto	poner – puesto	romper - roto

Using the preterite and the perfect tense

Use the preterite in Spanish when you'd use the *I ate* past tense in English, and the perfect tense when you'd say *I have eaten* in English.

The pluperfect tense (to say I *had* done something) is made using the imperfect instead of the present of *haber* before the past participle: Había, habías, había, habíamos, habíais, habían

Test yourself on the perfect and pluperfect tenses

1. He hablado en español y he leído el periódico.
2. Has comido todo el chocolate y has bebido el café.
3. Han vuelto a casa y han ayudado mucho.
4. Ha trabajado todo el día, pero ha roto el ordenador.
5. Hemos hecho todo, hemos abierto el restaurante y hemos puesto las mesas.
6. He visto la tele y he escrito una carta.
7. Cuando llegué ya habían salido.
8. Había estudiado mucho así que saqué buenas notas.

Answers

1. I have spoken Spanish and I have read the paper.
2. You have eaten all the chocolate and drunk all the coffee.
3. They have come home and have helped a lot.
4. S/he has worked all day but has broken the computer.
5. We have done everything, we have opened the restaurant and laid the tables.
6. I have watched TV and written a letter.
7. When I arrived they had already gone out.
8. I had studied a lot so I got good grades.

Vocabulary

Holidays

ir de vacaciones	to go on holiday
el año pasado	last year
el año próximo	next year
hace cinco años	5 years ago
reservar	to book/reserve
una habitación	a room
un hotel	a hotel

Getting there

fui a …. con ….	I went to…. with…..
pasé dos semanas	I spent two weeks
durante dos semanas	for two weeks
el viaje	the journey *(voyage)*
en el extranjero	abroad *(strangers)*
el vuelo duró	the flight lasted
hacer las maletas	to pack the suitcases
deshacer las maletas	to unpack the suitcases
el equipaje	the luggage
seguro /-a	sure, safe
la seguridad	security *(-dad ending = ity)*

Accommodation

alojarse	to stay *(lodge yourself)*
el alojamiento	accommodation

un apartamento	a flat
un albergue	a hostel
un camping	a campsite
el hotel estaba	the hotel was situated
cerca de la playa	near the beach
la arena	the sand *(from sandy arenas)*
la entrada	entrance
la salida	exit / departure
la vista	view
llegar	to arrive *(on your legs)*
había	there were / there was

Things to do on holiday

se puede	one can
probar actividades nuevas	to try new activities
sacar fotos	to take photos
probar los platos típicos	to try the local food
tomar el sol	to sunbathe
enviar postales	to send postcards
comprar recuerdos	to buy souvenirs *(a record)*
relajarse	to relax
descansar	to relax
divertirse	to have fun
conocer a gente nueva	to meet new people
salir a bailar	to go out dancing

Holiday positives

Lo pasé bomba	I had a great time
tengo ganas de	I would like to
volver	to go back
en el futuro	in the future
esperar	to hope / wait for
esperar con ganas	to look forward to
lo bueno fue que	the good thing was that
hizo sol	it was sunny
lo mejor fue	the best thing was
inolvidable	unforgettable

Holiday negatives

lo malo fue que	the bad thing was that
hizo frio	it was cold
perdí mi pasaporte	I lost my passport
olvidé los billetes	I forgot the tickets
perdió su móvil	he / she lost his / her mobile
me di cuenta	I realised
había perdido	I had lost
había dejado mi móvil	I had left my mobile
perdí el avión	I missed the plane *(lost it)*
el retraso	the delay
lo peor	the worst thing
tuve un accidente	I had an accident
tuve que ir al hospital	I had to go to hospital

Weather

hace sol	it's sunny
hace calor	it's hot
hace frio	it's cold
hace viento	it's windy
llueve	it's raining
hay tormentas	it is stormy
hay niebla	it's foggy
nieva	it's snowing
la lluvia	rain
las nubes	clouds
el cielo	the sky

Festivals

las fiestas	festivals
el Año Nuevo	New Year
la Navidad	Christmas
el árbol de Navidad	Christmas tree
la boda	wedding
el nacimiento	birth
la Nochebuena	Christmas Eve
la Nochevieja	New Year's Eve
la Pascua	Easter
mandar	to send
postales de Navidad	Christmas cards
encender velas	to light candles

un desfile	a procession
dar / recibir	to give / receive
regalos	presents
comemos	we eat
bebemos	we drink
jugamos a juegos	we play games
visito a mis abuelos	I visit my grandparents
damos regalos	we give presents
recibimos regalos	we receive presents
mi regalo favorito fue	my favourite present was
celebramos	we celebrate
vemos la tele	we watch TV
nos divertimos	we have fun
descansamos	we relax
nos relajamos	we relax
nos reímos	we laugh
vienen a vernos	they come to see us
vamos a verlos	we go to see them
no nos vemos mucho	we don't see each other much
pasamos tiempo juntos	we spend time together
aprovechamos	we make the most of

Eating meals

comer	to eat
desayunar	to have breakfast
desayuno tostadas	I have toast for breakfast

almorzar	to have lunch
el almuerzo	lunch
cenar	to have dinner
la cena	dinner
la merienda	tea
pedir	to ask for
probar	to try
la cocina	cooking / the kitchen
cocinar	to cook

General food

pan	bread
tostadas	toast
cereales	cereal
mantequilla	butter *(meant-to-kill-ya)*
mermelada	jam
bocadillos	sandwiches
el arroz	rice
el queso	cheese
los alimentos	food
la comida	food

la carne	**meat**
el pollo	chicken
un bistec	a steak
la carne de ternera	beef

el cerdo	pig / pork
el cordero	lamb
una chuleta	a chop
el jamón	ham
la ternera	veal
una hamburguesa	a hamburger
pescado	fish

las verduras	vegetables
las judías verdes	green beans
el pimiento	pepper
los guisantes	peas
la ensalada	salad
los champiñones	mushrooms (*champions*)
la lechuga	lettuce
el tomate	tomato
las zanahorias	carrots (bigger *than-your-ears*)
las espinacas	spinach
el espárrago	asparagus
la coliflor	cauliflower
las patatas	potatoes
las patatas fritas	chips
el pepino	cucumber
las cebollas	onions (*they-boil-ya*)

las frutas	fruit
la naranja	orange
las uvas	grapes
la cereza	cherry
el limón	lemon
las manzanas	apples *(man has Adam's apple)*
el plátano	banana *(curls around a plate)*
el melocotón	peach *(peach skin feels cotton)*
la pera	pear
la piña	pineapple
el albaricoque	apricot
el helado	ice cream
caramelos	sweets
pasteles	cakes
las bebidas	drinks
una cerveza	beer
la leche	milk
un té	tea
un café	coffee
un vino tinto	red wine
un vino blanco	white wine
el agua	water
zumo	juice
una limonado	lemonade
cubitos de hielo	ice cubes

en el restaurante	in the restaurant
los platos	plates
el tenedor	fork
la cuchara	spoon
el cuchillo	knife
el vaso	a glass
el camarero	waiter
la cuenta	the bill
la propina	the tip

How much can you remember?

1. Recite the preterite of *hablar*, *comer* and *vivir*

2. When do we use the preterite and the perfect tense?

3. How is the perfect tense constructed?

4. What are the main irregular past participles?

For your oral and writing

The standard story about a day out

This story is verb-heavy. I haven't used *fui* more than once – but I've brought in some friends so I can use *fuimos* instead. In the restaurant, I have mentioned what I ate, what they ate and what we ate, to maximise verb potential, and I have used *tomar* as well as *comer* to spice it up. Also, make sure you say you *had to* do something rather than you just did it, because it will enrich your writing and speaking.

El fin de semana pasado fui al centro comercial para comprar un regalo para mi madre porque fue su cumpleaños. Compré un libro porque le gusta leer. Después mis amigos y yo fuimos al cine para ver una película, y al llegar compramos entradas y caramelos. En mi opinión la película fue fenomenal pero un poco larga. Después de ver la película comimos en un restaurante. Comí pizza, mis amigos comieron pasta y después tomamos helados. Fue delicioso y me gustó mucho. Luego volvimos a la casa de mi amigo para jugar al futbol en el jardín, y antes de acostarme tuve que hacer mis deberes.

Last weekend I went to the shopping centre to buy a present for my mother because it was her birthday. I bought her a book because she likes reading. Then my friends and I went to see a film, and on arriving we bought tickets and sweets. In my opinion the film was great but a bit long. After watching the film we ate in a restaurant. I ate pizza and my friends ate pasta. Then we had ice cream. It was delicious and I liked it a lot. Then we went back to my friend's house to play football in the garden and before going to bed I had to do my homework.

A memorable day

Decidí organizar un partido de futbol entre los profes y los alumnos para recaudar fondos para libros nuevos para la biblioteca. Vendí los billetes en línea porque es rápido y fácil. Después de venderlos, fui al supermercado con mis amigos para comprar caramelos, bocadillos y bebidas que vendimos durante el partido. Recaudamos muchísimo dinero y pudimos comprar todos los libros que necesitábamos. Además, los alumnos ganaron el partido. ¡Que suerte!

I decided to organize a football match between the teachers and the pupils to raise funds for new books for the library. I sold the tickets online because it's quick and easy. After selling them we went to the supermarket with my friends to buy sweets, sandwiches and drinks which we sold during the match. We raised lots of money and were able to buy all the books which we needed. Also the pupils won the match. How lucky!

The last film you saw

Acabo de ver Titanic y fue estupendo. Trata de dos jóvenes amantes que cruzan sus destinos en el viaje inaugural del crucero Titanic. Pero cuando el crucero choca con un iceberg en el gélido Océano Atlántico Norte, su apasionado encuentro amoroso se convierte en una desesperada carrera por sobrevivir.

I have just watched Titanic and it was great. It is about two young lovers whose destinies cross on the inaugural journey of the cruise ship Titanic. But when the ship hits an iceberg in the frozen North Atlantic their passionate encounter becomes a desperate race to survive.

Yesterday at school

Ayer fui al cole en autobús y al llegar, charlé con mis amigos. Las clases empezaron a las nueve y tuve cinco clases de cuarenta minutos antes de la comida. Durante el recreo a las diez y veinte, comí una galleta y jugué al baloncesto.

Durante la hora de comer, comimos en el comedor y después fui al club de teatro porque es mi pasatiempo favorito. Las clases terminaron a las cuatro y volví a casa para cenar y hacer mis deberes.

Yesterday I went to school by bus and when I arrived I chatted with my friends. Lessons began at 9 and I had 5 classes of 40 minutes each before lunch. During break at 10.20 I ate a biscuit and played basketball. During the lunch hour we ate in the canteen and afterwards I went to drama club because it's my favourite hobby. Lessons finished at 4 and I went home to have dinner and do my homework.

Last Christmas

El año pasado, mis abuelos vinieron a vernos y pasamos el día juntos, comiendo, bebiendo, hablando y jugando. Recibí un montón de regalos. ¡Qué bueno! Después de una comida riquísima vimos la televisión y mi abuelo se durmió en el sofá. Antes de acostarnos jugamos a las cartas, pero mi padre tocó el piano y tuvimos que taparnos los oídos.

Last year my grandparents came to see us and we spent the day together, eating, drinking, talking and playing. I received loads of presents. How great! After a delicious meal we watched television and my grandfather fell asleep on the sofa. Before going to bed we played cards but my father played the piano and we had to block our ears.

Last year's holiday

Tengo suerte porque hace un año, fui a ………………….. en …barco / coche / avión con …una amiga / unas amigas / un amigo / unos amigos / mi familia. Pasé ……………….. días / semanas / meses relajándome. Nos alojamos en un hotel cerca de la playa. Tomé el sol, hice equitación, jugué al tenis, nadé en el mar, visité monumentos históricos, descansé, leí libros, conocí a gente nueva, dormí mucho. Hizo sol todos los días. Fue fenomenal. ¡Lo pasé bomba!

I am lucky because a year ago I went to ....by boat / car / plane with a friend / with friends / with my family. I spent .... days /weeks / months relaxing. We stayed in a hotel near the beach. I sunbathed, went horseriding, played tennis, swam in the sea, visited historical sites, relaxed, read books, met new people, slept a lot. It was sunny every day. It was amazing. I had a great time.

Importance of holidays

Las vacaciones son importantes por muchas razones. Primero tenemos que relajarnos después del trabajo cuando hemos currado un montón. También es importante conocer la cultura de los países extranjeros para que podamos tener un mejor entendimiento sobre la gente del mundo. Además, se puede aprovechar la oportunidad de aprender nuevos deportes y probar nuevas actividades por primera vez.

Holidays are important for many reasons. Firstly, we need to relax after work when we have been working our socks off. Also, it's important to get to know the culture of foreign countries so that we can have a better understanding of the people of the world. Moreover, you can learn new sports and take the opportunity to try new activities for the first time.

Festivals in England

No hay muchas fiestas in Inglaterra. La única fiesta que celebramos en nuestra familia es la Navidad, mientras que en España hay un montón de fiestas durante todo el año. La mayoría son religiosas, pero también hay fiestas divertidas como la Tomatina cerca de Valencia, donde los participantes se arrojan tomates los unos a los otros. Si solo pudiéramos tener batallas de tomates aquí en Inglaterra. Claro que tenemos fiestas de arte y de música como en todos los países. No obstante, las fiestas de música cuestan un ojo de la cara.

There aren't many festivals in England. The only festival we celebrate in our family is Christmas, whereas in Spain there are loads of festivals all year round. Most of them are religious but there are also fun festivals like the Tomatina near Valencia where they throw tomatoes at each other. If only we had tomato battles here in England... Of course, we have art and music festivals as all countries do. However, music festivals cost a fortune.

Help at home yesterday

Ayer lavé los platos, puse la mesa y arreglé mi dormitorio. Habría hecho más si hubiera tenido tiempo, pero los profes nos dan demasiados deberes.

Yesterday I washed the dishes, laid the table and tidied my room. I would have done more if I had had time, but the teachers give us too much homework.

This morning

Hoy me pegué un madrugón porque tuve que ir al colegio, me duché, me vestí y desayuné de prisa antes de irme. Siempre tengo prisa por la mañana. Fui al colegio en autobús y llegué a las ocho. Al llegar, charlé con mis amigos e hice un poco más de repaso para mi examen oral de español.

Today I got up really early because I had to go to school. I showered, got dressed and had breakfast quickly before leaving. I am always in a hurry in the morning. I went to school by bus and arrived at 8. I chatted with my friends and did a bit more revision for my Spanish oral exam.

NOTES

Day 5

(You're half way there – this is a short day, so after completing the chapter, go back and revise days 1-4)

In this session you will be revising:

- The imperfect tense
- Vocabulary relating to transport
- Oral and written answers that use the imperfect tense

The imperfect tense

This tense is used mainly to describe what used to happen in the past, rather than one-off events where you use the preterite or the perfect tense.

Hablar (to speak)	**Comer** (to eat)	**Vivir** (to live)
hablaba	comía	vivía
hablabas	comías	vivías
hablaba	comía	vivía
hablábamos	comíamos	vivíamos
hablabais	comíais	vivíais
hablaban	comían	vivían

There are only three exceptions:

Ser – era (I used to be)

Ir – iba (I used to go)

Ver – veía (I used to watch / see)

Here is a passage that shows the use of the three past tenses, the perfect, preterite and imperfect

He visitado muchos países. Cuando era pequeña, iba a España cada año. Me gustaba mucho porque había mucho que hacer y hacía sol todo el tiempo. Pero el año pasado fuimos a Francia. Pasé dos semanas en la playa pero no me gustaba nada porque no podía hablar español.

I have visited many countries. When I was little we went to Spain every year. I liked it because there was lots to do and it was sunny all the time. But last year we went to France. I spent two weeks on the beach but I didn't like it at all because I wasn't able to speak Spanish.

The imperfect tense is used:

- To describe an action in the past that you used to do (**repeated**)
  Cuando era joven hacia natación todos los días.
  When *I was* young *I went swimming* every day.

- To say "it was" (era) and "there was" (había)

- To describe what *was* going on
  Estaba lloviendo   it was raining
  Estaba trabajando   I was working
  Estaba feliz   I was happy

Practise the imperfect tense...

I used to play tennis   jugaba al tenis

I went cycling every day   hacía ciclismo todos los días

I had a dog   tenía un perro

I wanted to have a rabbit   quería un conejo

There was a cinema in town   había un cine en la ciudad

There wasn't a pool   no había piscina

I was happy   estaba content / feliz

I couldn't go out   no podía salir

Vocabulary

Transport

el transporte público	public transport
en autobús	by bus
en tren	by train
en coche	by car
en barco	by boat
en bici	by bike
en avión	by plane *(aviation)*
la estación de trenes	the train station
tomar el tren	to take the train
en el andén	on the platform
comprar billetes	to buy tickets
un billete de ida y vuelta	return ticket
la taquilla	ticket office
la consigna	left luggage office
subir al tren	to get on the train
subir al taxi	to get in the taxi
bajar del tren	to get off the train
bajar del taxi	to get out of the taxi
perdí el tren	I missed the train
a pie	on foot
voy andando	I walk
caro	expensive *(expensive car)*
barato	cheap *(cheap bar)*
la parada de autobuses	the bus stop

rutas para ciclistas	cycle paths
una red de transporte	a transport network
tardo una hora en ir al…	it takes me an hour to get to…

What can you remember?

1. When do we use the imperfect tense?

2. What are the endings?

3. How do you say *it was* and *there was*?

For your oral and writing

Hobbies when you were young

Cuando era joven hacía un poco menos deporte, pero pasaba la mayoría del tiempo en el parque cerca de mi casa, jugando con mis amigos, así que mantenía la forma sin esforzarme. También, veía la tele todos los días y jugaba los videojuegos. Solía leer mucho también.

When I was young I did slightly less sport but I spent the majority of my time in the park near my house, playing with friends so I kept in shape without making any effort. Also, I watched the television every day and played videogames. I used to read a lot as well.

Primary school

Cuando era joven iba a una escuela primaria cerca de mi casa. Los profes eran simpáticos y no nos daban tantos deberes que ahora. ¡Qué bueno! Había un gran jardín donde solíamos jugar durante el recreo. Lo malo era que no me gustaba la comida escolar porque nos daban demasiadas verduras.

When I was young, I went to a primary school near my house. The teachers were nice and didn't give us as much homework as they do now. How great! There was a big garden where we used to play at breaktime. The bad thing was that I didn't like the school dinners because they gave us too many vegetables.

Day 6

In this session you will be revising:

- The near future tense
- The simple future tense
- Vocabulary relating to education and jobs
- Oral and written answers on education, jobs and future plans

The near future tense

This is the easiest tense to use as it relies on conjugating only one verb – the verb *ir* – to go:

Voy a ir a España – I'm going to go to Spain

Vamos a comer pasta – We are going to eat pasta

ir = to go

voy	I go (or am going)
vas	you go
va	he / she / it goes
vamos	we go
vais	you (plural) go
van	they go

Examples of this future tense in action – don't forget the a

No vamos a salir	We are not going to go out
Van a trabajar	They are going to work
Vamos a comer tapas	We are going to eat tapas
Voy a visitar sitios turísticos	I'm going to visit tourist sights
Van a ir a la playa	They are going to go to the beach
Voy a dormir	I am going to sleep
¿Vas a jugar?	Are you going to play?
¿Vais a ir?	Are you (pl) going to go?
¿No vas a venir?	Aren't you going to come?
No voy a beber	I'm not going to drink
Vamos a ver…	We shall see…

The simple future tense

Hablar (to speak)	Comer (to eat)	Vivir (to live)
hablaré	comeré	viviré
hablarás	comerás	vivirás
hablará	comerá	vivirá
hablaremos	comeremos	viviremos
hablaréis	comeréis	viviréis
hablarán	comerán	vivirán

The good thing is that the endings are the same for all verbs, and you can recite them to learn them, beginning with RE which is also the last two letters of the word *future*. This tense must be used in your writing and speaking as well as the near future. Don't think too much about when to use which one. A general mish-mash of both will usually do. The thing is to watch out for the exceptions to the rule that the future root is the infinitive:

tener	tendré	I will have
salir	saldré	I will go out
hacer	haré	I will do / make
poner	pondré	I will put
haber	habrá	there will be
decir	diré	I will say
poder	podré	I will be able to
venir	vendré	I will come
querer	querré	I will want
saber	sabré	I will know

Test on the simple future

1. They will help their parents

2. We will work hard

3. I will do my homework

4. They will eat a lot of tapas

5. I will go out with my friends to the cinema

6. He will go to the beach

7. I will play tennis with my brother

8. I will have to get up early

9. My grandparents will come tomorrow

10. There will be two swimming pools

Answers

1. Ayudarán a sus padres

2. Trabajaremos duro

3. Haré mis deberes

4. Comerán muchas tapas

5. Saldré con mis amigos al cine

6. Irá a la playa

7. Jugaré al tenis con mi hermano

8. Tendré que levantarme temprano

9. Mis abuelos vendrán mañana

10. Habrá dos piscinas

Vocabulary

School and lessons

un colegio	a school
un insti	a school
mi escuela primaria	my primary school
un internado	boarding school
una escuela de niñas	a girls' school
una escuela de niños	a boys' school

School positives

el mejor colegio	the best school
del mundo	in the world
lo que más me gusta	what I like most
los profes son buenos	the teachers are good
los alumnos	the pupils
mucho que hacer	lots to do
tengo muchos amigos	I have lots of friends

School negatives

lo que no me gusta	what I don't like
tenemos que	we have to
llevar un uniforme	wear a uniform
los profes nos dan	the teachers give us
demasiados deberes	too much homework
las reglas son estrictas	the rules are strict
no se puede	you can't

comer chicle	to chew gum
usar el móvil	to use a mobile
llevar joyas	to wear jewellery
llevar maquillaje	to wear make-up

Facilities

aulas	classrooms *(teacher = wise owl)*
laboratorios	laboratories
una biblioteca	a library
un comedor	a dining room
campos deportivos	sports fields
una piscina	a pool
el patio	the playground
donde se puede	where you can
paso tiempo leyendo	I spend time reading
jugar	to play
charlar	to chat
estudiar	to study

Subjects

las matemáticas	maths
(las) ciencias	sciences
la biología	biology
la química	chemistry
la física	physics
la música	music

la geografía	geography
la historia	history
el francés	French
el inglés	English
el latín	Latin

Education verbs

enseñar	to teach *(you need to be 'senior')*
aprender	to learn *(an apprentice learns)*
sacar buenas notas	to get good marks *(out of the sack)*
tener éxito	to succeed *(exciting!)*
repasar	to revise
pasar exámenes	to take exams
aprobar un examen	to pass an exam *(probably?)*
sacarse un reprobado	to fail (*reprobate!*)
preguntar	to ask
contestar	to answer *(in a contest)*
poner pruebas	to give tests

School day

al llegar	on arriving
a las ocho	at 8 o'clock
las clases empiezan	lessons begin
cada clase dura	each lesson lasts
ocho clases al día	eight lessons a day
la hora de comer	the lunch hour

el descanso	break time
el recreo	break time
las clases terminan	lessons finish
vuelvo a casa	I go home

Plans for the future

seguir estudiando	to carry on studying
para que pueda	so that I can
conseguir un buen trabajo	get a good job
cuando sea mayor	when I'm older
ayudar a la gente	to help people
ganar mucho dinero	to earn a lot
viajar por todas partes	to travel everywhere
cambiar el mundo	to change the world
sobre todo	especially
trabajo voluntario	voluntary work
una organización benéfica	a charity

Jobs

un empleo / un trabajo	job
azafata	air hostess
contable	accountant
abogado / -a	lawyer
hombre / mujer de negocios	businessman / businesswoman
profesor /-a	teacher
científico /-a	scientist

peluquero /-a	hairdresser
periodista	journalist
enfermero /-a	nurse
marinero /-a	sailor
escultor /-a	sculptor
escritor /-a	writer
pescador /-a	fisherman
bombero /-a	fireman
panadero /-a	baker
matador	bullfighter
ingeniero /-a	engineer
cantante	singer

Part time jobs

a tiempo parcial	part-time
experiencia laboral	work experience
ganar un sueldo	to earn a salary
trabajaba	I used to work
ganaba	I uscd to earn
tenía que	I had to
poner las mesas	to lay the tables
preparar las verduras	to prepare the vegetables
limpiar la cocina	to clean the kitchen
servir a los clientes	to serve the customers
recibía propinas	I used to get tips
ahorré mi dinero	I saved my money

un aprendizaje	apprenticeship
una compañía	a company
una empresa	a business

How much can you remember?

1. How does the verb *ir* go in the present tense?

2. What is it followed by to make the near future tense?

3. What are the simple future tense endings?

4. Which verbs take an irregular future root?

5. What is that irregular root?

For your oral and writing

Future tense answers

When answering a question about your future, look out for an opportunity to use a few key expressions which show off a high level of Spanish. These are:

- **Cuando sea mayor** - when I am older
  (This expression uses the subjunctive of *ser* and ticks a box showing knowledge of an important grammar rule.)

- **Voy a seguir haciendo deporte / reciclando / estudiando** – I'm going to carry on doing sport / recycling / studying
  (The verb seguir + gerund)

- **Aunque sea difícil / aburrido / caro** – although it's difficult / boring / expensive
  Aunque is another expression requiring the subjunctive in most cases.

- **Para que pueda ser / aprovechar / salvar / trabajar** – so that I can be / make the most of / save / work
  Para que is also followed by the subjunctive.

Example sentence about the future
Cuando sea mayor voy a seguir estudiando español, aunque sea difícil, para que pueda trabajar en España.

When I'm older I'm going to carry on studying Spanish, although it's difficult, so that I can work in Spain.

You can adapt this to fit the health or environment topics, saying what you're going to continue doing and why.

Where will you live in the future?

Cuando sea mayor, voy a seguir viviendo en Londres para que pueda aprovechar todas las actividades y quedarme cerca de mis amigos. Viviré en una casa moderna y grande, bien equipada, con vistas bonitas. Es importante que haya suficiente espacio para fiestas porque me encanta bailar.

When I'm older I will continue living in London so I can make the most of all the activities and stay close to my friends. I will live in a modern, large, well-appointed house with pretty views. It is important that there is enough space for parties because I love dancing.

This evening

Al llegar a casa voy a relajarme antes de hacer mis deberes. Veré la tele e intentaré olvidar el estrés del día escolar. ¡Ojalá pudiera! Cenaré sobre las siete. Después charlaré con mis compañeros de clase en las redes sociales, porque soy adicto y no puedo prescindir de Facebook y Snapchat.

When I get home I'm going to relax before doing my homework. I will watch TV and I will try to forget the stress of the school day. If only I could! I will have dinner around 7. Afterwards I will chat with my school friends on social networks because I am addicted and I can't manage without Facebook and Snapchat.

Plans for next weekend with family

El fin de semana que viene, me gustaría hacer ciclismo con mi padre porque nos gusta pasar tiempo al aire libre. Por la tarde voy a ir de compras con mi madre. Después iremos al cine para ver la nueva película de James Bond porque nos encantan las películas de acción. Antes de volver a casa cenaremos en un restaurante y discutiremos la película. Al llegar a casa me acostaré y dormiré como un tronco.

Next weekend I'd like to go cycling with my dad because we like spending time in the fresh air. In the afternoon I'm going to go shopping with my mother. Afterwards we will go to the cinema to see the new Bond film because we love action films.

Before going home, we will have dinner in a restaurant and discuss the film. When I get home I will go to bed and sleep like a log.

Future holiday

El año que viene / cuando haya terminado mis exámenes, iré a Grecia con mi familia y unos amigos. Nos alojaremos en un hotel cerca de la playa y vamos a jugar al tenis todos los días. Tomaré el sol, nadaré en el mar y descansaré porque tendré que relajarme después de los exámenes. Espero con ganas las vacaciones.

Next year / when I have finished my exams, I will go to Greece with my family and some friends. We will stay in a hotel near the beach and we are going to play tennis every day. I will sunbathe, swim in the sea and relax because I will need to rest after the exams. I am looking forward to it.

Next Christmas

Este año mis abuelos van a venir a vernos, y pasaremos el día juntos, comiendo, bebiendo, hablando y jugando. Recibiré un montón de regalos. ¡Qué bueno! Después de una comida riquísima veremos la televisión y mi abuelo se dormirá en el sofá. Antes de acostarnos jugaremos a las cartas, mi padre tocará el piano y tendremos que taparnos los oídos.

Next year my grandparents will come to see us and we will spend the day together, eating, drinking, talking and playing. I will get loads of presents. How great! After a delicious meal we will watch television and my grandfather will fall asleep on the sofa. Before going to bed we will play cards, my father will play the piano and we will have to block our ears.

The future of mobile phones

En el futuro, creo que los móviles se volverán más finos con pantallas más grandes y útiles. Pero pase lo que pase tendrán más potencia y deberemos tener cuidado con la información que compartimos por internet porque corremos el riesgo de ser víctimas de delito informático.

In the future, I believe that mobiles with become thinner with bigger, more useful screens and more useful. But whatever happens they will be more powerful and we will have to be careful with the information we share on the internet because we risk being victims of cybercrime.

The education topic

(Remember to use chapter 2 to remind you how to describe your school.)

Likes and dislikes about school

Me gusta mi colegio porque tengo muchos amigos, pero lo que no me gusta es que los profes nos dan demasiados deberes. También, si hubiera una piscina / un cine, estaría contentísimo. Si pudiera cambiar algo, cambiaría el uniforme porque es incómodo y feo. Estoy harto de él.

I like my school because I have lots of friends but what I don't like is that the teachers give us too much homework. Also if there was a pool / a cinema I would be very happy. If I could change something I would change the uniform because it's uncomfortable and ugly. I'm sick of it.

School day

Las clases empiezan a las nueve y terminan a las cuatro. Tenemos seis clases al día y cada clase dura una hora. Durante el recreo, juego con mis amigos y como un bocadillo. A menudo voy a un club durante la hora de comer. A veces voy al colegio andando, pero normalmente voy en coche y vuelvo en tren. Suelo hacer dos horas de deberes por la tarde.

Lessons begin at 9 and finish at 4. We have 6 lessons a day and each one lasts an hour. During break time I play with my friends and eat a sandwich. I often go to a club at lunchtime. Sometimes I walk to school but normally I go to school by car and come back by train. I usually do two hours of homework in the evening.

Subjects

Estoy estudiando francés, español, dibujo, latín, inglés, deporte, ciencias, matemáticas, música, historia y geografía. Mi asignatura favorita es ....porque el profe es simpático y saco buenas notas. No me gusta el latín porque es difícil, el profe es aburrido y el profe nos da demasiados deberes.

I am studying French, Spanish, art, Latin, English, sport, sciences, maths, music, history and geography. My favourite subject is ..... because the teacher is nice and I get good marks. I don't like Latin because it's difficult, the teacher is boring and the teacher gives us too much homework.

Describe your uniform

Tenemos que llevar un uniforme: [una falda negra, una camisa blanca, pantalones negros, una chaqueta negra, zapatos negros, calcetines o medias, una corbata y un jersey]. Si pudiera cambiar algo, cambiaría el uniforme porque es incómodo y feo. Estoy harto de él.

We have to wear a uniform – [a black skirt, a white shirt, black trousers, a black jacket, black shoes, socks or tights, a tie and a jumper]. If I could change something, I would change the uniform because it's uncomfortable and ugly. I'm sick of it.

Opinion of uniform

Claro que hay ventajas de llevar un uniforme. No tienes que pensar en lo que vas a ponerte por la mañana y no hay presión de vestirse de moda. Todos se parecen y así se puede evitar el acoso escolar. No obstante, en mi colegio, si pudiera cambiar algo, cambiaría el uniforme porque es incómodo y feo. Estoy harto de él.

Of course there are advantages to wearing a uniform. You don't have to think about what you are going to wear in the morning and there is no pressure to dress in a fashionable way. Everyone looks the same and in this way you can avoid bullying in schools. However, if I could change something in my school I would change the uniform because it's uncomfortable and ugly. I'm sick of it.

Opinion of homework

Aunque sean útiles para comprender lo que hemos aprendido en el colegio, los deberes me molestan porque los profes nos dan demasiados. Yo tengo dos horas de deberes al día y estoy siempre agotado. Si no los hubiera, por lo menos durante la semana, sería mucho mejor.

Although it's useful for understanding what we have learnt in class, homework annoys me because the teachers give us too much. I have two hours of homework per day and I'm always exhausted! If we didn't have any, at least during the week, it would be much better.

School rules

Las reglas son bastante estrictas. Por ejemplo, no se puede usar el móvil durante las clases; tampoco se puede comer chicle. Si charlamos, los profes se enfadan. Ayer me castigaron por hablar en clase y tuve que quedarme en el colegio hasta las cinco de la tarde. El maquillaje está prohibido pero las chicas lo ponen de todas formas.

The rules are quite strict. For example, you can't use your phone during lessons; you can't chew gum either. If we chat, the teachers get cross. Yesterday I got a detention for talking in class and had to stay at school until 5pm. Make-up isn't allowed but the girls wear it anyway.

Spanish and English schools

Parece que los colegios españoles son menos estrictos que los colegios ingleses. No tienen uniforme y el ambiente en el colegio es mucho más agradable porque los alumnos no tienen miedo de los profes. Mi amiga española me dijo que no tiene exámenes cada año como nosotros. ¡Qué suerte! Tengo tanta envidia de los estudiantes españoles. Lo malo es que, al fin y al cabo, parece que los estudiantes españoles no tienen tanto éxito como nosotros al terminar el colegio, y el desempleo va aumentando entre los jóvenes españoles.

It seems that Spanish schools are less strict than English schools. They don't have uniform and the atmosphere in the school is much nicer because the pupils are not scared of the teachers. My Spanish friend told me that she doesn't have exams every year like we do. How lucky! I am so jealous of the Spanish students. The bad thing is that at the end of the day, it seems that Spanish students are less successful than us after school and unemployment is rising amongst Spanish young people.

Part-time job / work experience

El año pasado pasé una semana trabajando en un colegio y me gustó mucho, pero he currado un montón y no gané nada. Ahora tengo un trabajo a tiempo parcial desde hace dos meses en un restaurante en mi barrio que se llama Pizza Mama y es harina de otro costal. Trabajo el sábado desde las dos hasta las seis de la tarde. Trabajo en la cocina, lavando los platos y preparando las verduras y las ensaladas. En el restaurante mismo, pongo las mesas y sirvo a los clientes. Lo que más me gusta es el dinero porque los clientes siempre me dan propinas enormes. ¡Me lo paso bomba!

Last year I spent a week working in a school and I liked it a lot but I worked my socks off and earned nothing. Now I have had a part time job for the past two months in a restaurant in my area called Pizza Mama and it's something else entirely. I work on Saturdays from 2 till 6. I work in the kitchen washing dishes and preparing vegetables and salads. In the restaurant itself I lay the tables and serve customers. What I like most is the money because the customers always give huge tips. I have a great time!

Future education

El año que viene voy a seguir estudiando inglés, historia y matemáticas porque son mis asignaturas favoritas. Dejaré las ciencias porque me aburren. Trabajaré duro para que pueda ir a una buena universidad, donde espero estudiar derecho.

Next year I am going to carry on studying English, history and maths because they are my favourite subjects. I will give up sciences because they bore me. I will work hard so I can go to a good university, where I hope to study law.

Future job

No sé exactamente qué voy a hacer cuando sea mayor. Lo importante es que sea interesante. Me gustaría hacerme profe de historia porque es mi asignatura favorita y los profes tienen suerte porque no trabajan durante el verano.

I don't know exactly what I want to do when I'm older. The important thing is that it is interesting. I would like to become a history teacher because it's my favourite subject, and teachers are lucky because they don't work during the summer.

Day 7

In this session you will be revising:

- The conditional tense
- How to talk about the ideal
- Vocabulary relating to technology
- Oral and written answers on the technology topic

The conditional tense *(I would…)*

Hablar (to speak)	Comer (to eat)	Vivir (to live)
hablaría	comería	viviría
hablarías	comerías	vivirías
hablaría	comería	viviría
hablaríamos	comeríamos	viviríamos
hablaríais	comeríais	viviríais
hablarían	comerían	vivirían

The endings go on the future root, which is usually the infinitive unless it's one of the irregulars on the list above. This tense is the "would" tense, so use it where you would say "would" in English.

Viviría en Londres	I *would* live in London
Comería muchas verduras	I *would* eat lots of vegetables
Haría más ejercicio	I *would* do more exercise

The tricky bit about conditional sentences

For the beginning of this type of sentence, you will need the past subjunctive. Don't worry too much about its formation, (the root is the third person plural of the preterite, for those who want to know) but the key phrases you need for GCSE are:

Si hubiera más rutas para ciclistas	If there were more cycle paths
Si pudiera cambiar algo	If I could change something
Si fuera alcalde / madre / rico	If I were mayor / a mother / rich
Si tuviera mucho dinero	If I had lots of money

Now add your conditional verb on the end, to form an *if* sentence.

Test yourself

1. If I could change something, I would change the uniform.

2. If there were more cycle paths, I'd go to school by bike.

3. If it were possible, I'd get up at ten.

4. If there were a swimming pool, I'd be happy.

5. If I had lots of money, I'd live in New York.

Answers

1. Si pudiera cambiar algo, cambiaría el uniforme.

2. Si hubiera más rutas para ciclistas, iría al colegio en bici.

3. Si fuera posible, me levantaría a las diez.

4. Si hubiera una piscina, estaría contento.

5. Si tuviera mucho dinero, viviría en Nueva York.

Expert level *if* sentences

Even if you just learn and use one of these, you will make an examiner smile. When you talk about a shopping trip or a holiday, Christmas, birthdays, or any event where money is spent, you can add *If I had had more money I would have bought more presents.* This is how you say it in Spanish:

Si hubiera tenido más dinero, habría comprado más regalos.

The structure is similar to the perfect and pluperfect tenses – a form of the verb *haber* followed by the past participle. What could be simpler?

Vocabulary

Technology

la tecnología	technology
soy adicto	I'm addicted
no puedo prescindir de	I can't do without
el móvil	the mobile phone
el ordenador	the computer
enviar mensajes	to send messages
ponerse al día	to get up to date
navegar por internet	to surf the internet
descargar	to download
colgar	to post
borrar	to delete
guardar	to save
grabar	to record
películas y música	films and music
las redes sociales	social networks
una página web	a website
ponerse en contacto con	to get in touch with
buscar información	to look up information

Technology dangers

Hablar con desconocidos	to talk to strangers
problemas de vista	eyesight problems
pegado a la pantalla	glued to the screen
perder amigos	to lose friends

volverse solitario	to get lonely
volverse triste	to get depressed
causar accidentes	to cause accidents
cruzas la calle mirándolo	you cross the road looking at it
se vuelven	they become
adicto(s)	addicted
obeso	obese
hay el riesgo de	there is the risk of
el robo de identidad	identity theft
ciber intimidación	cyber-bullying
la piratería	hacking

How much can you remember?

Where do we get the root to make the conditional?

What are the conditional endings?

Which other tense shares these endings?

For your oral and writing

La tecnología

La tecnología es útil por muchas razones. Tengo suerte porque acabo de recibir un móvil nuevo para mi cumpleaños.

Soy adicto.

Lo uso (I use it) para todo, para:

- Mantener contacto con mis padres
- Ayudar con mis deberes
- Mandar mensajes en las redes sociales
- Descargar música y películas
- Jugar en las aplicaciones

Pero hay muchos peligros – por ejemplo

- Muchos jóvenes se vuelven adictos
- Si cruzas la calle mirando la pantalla se puede fácilmente tener un accidente
- También hay el riesgo de robo de identidad y de ciber intimidación

El gobierno debería animar a los jóvenes a hacer más deporte y dejar los móviles en casa.

Technology is important for lots of reasons. I am lucky because I have just received a new mobile for my birthday, and I'm addicted to it. I use it for everything, for staying in touch with my parents, for helping with homework, to send messages on social networks, for downloading films and music and playing on the apps. However, there are lots of dangers. For example, lots of young people become addicted. If you cross the road while looking at the screen you can easily have an accident. Moreover, there is the risk of identity theft and cyber-bullying. The government should encourage young people to do more sport and leave their phones at home.

More on technology…

Do you watch TV?

Si, veo las telenovelas todos los días para relajarme, y porque me hacen reír y los vemos juntos, mis hermanos y yo. Además, nunca me pierdo los programas de deportes, especialmente los partidos de futbol. Veo las noticias de vez en cuando porque me informan y me interesan mucho. Si tuviera más tiempo vería más programas, pero los profes nos dan demasiados deberes.

Yes, I watch soap operas every day to relax and because they make me laugh and I watch them together with my brothers. In addition, I never miss sports programmes, especially football matches. I watch the news from time to time because it is informative and interesting. If I had more time I would watch more programmes but the teachers give us too much homework.

Young people and TV

Creo que si vemos la televisión corremos el riesgo de pasar demasiadas horas encerrados en casa. Puede crear adicción en algunas personas que pierden el control de las horas que pasan delante de la pequeña pantalla y por consiguiente pierden la capacidad de comunicarse cara a cara. Sin embargo, pienso que ver la televisión es mejor que los videojuegos y las redes sociales porque los documentales pueden ser una herramienta educativa ya que permiten que los jóvenes sean conscientes de problemas sociales y globales.

I believe that if we watch television we risk spending too much time stuck at home. It can create addiction in some people who lose control of the hours that they spend in front of the small screen and consequently lose the capacity to communicate face to face. However, I think that watching television is better than video games and social networks because documentaries can be an educational tool as they make young people aware of social and global problems.

Answers requiring the conditional tense

Ideal house

Si fuera rico me compraría mi casa ideal. Mi casa ideal sería enorme, moderna y cómoda, con una gran piscina para que pudiera hacer natación todos los días. Si fuera riquísima, habría también un cine donde pasaría muchísimas horas viendo películas con mis amigos, y un jardín con árboles y flores. Estaría cerca del centro de Londres para que mis amigos pudieran visitarme.

If I were rich, I would buy my ideal house. My ideal house would be enormous, modern and comfortable with a big pool so I could swim every day. If I was really rich there would also be a cinema where I would spend many hours watching films with my friends, and a garden with trees and flowers. It would be near the centre of London so that my friends could visit me.

Ideal family

No creo que exista la familia ideal. Lo importante es que el niño necesita el amor y la estabilidad, y el tipo de familia no importa. Lo importante es que puedas contar con tu familia. Hoy en día hay un montón de tipos de familia – con parejas homosexuales, familias monoparentales y tradicionales, familias numerosas, hijos únicos, y todos tienen su valor. Tengo suerte porque en mi familia nos llevamos bien.

I don't think there is such a thing as the ideal family – the important thing is that a child needs love and stability and the type of family doesn't matter. The important thing is to be able to rely on your family. Nowadays there are loads of different types of family – with homosexual couples, single parents, traditional families, large families and only children, and all have their value. I am lucky because in my family we get on well.

What you would change about your routine

Si fuera posible, no haría deberes durante la semana. Cada tarde tengo que hacer dos horas de deberes y estoy siempre cansado y estresado. Además, me gustaría quedarme acostado hasta más tarde. Los científicos dicen que los jóvenes necesitan dormir más y estoy completamente de acuerdo. El colegio debería empezar al mediodía.

If it were possible, I wouldn't do homework during the week. Every evening I have to do two hours of homework and I am always tired and stressed. Also, I would like to stay in bed until later. Scientists say that young people need more sleep and I am completely in agreement. School should start at midday.

Ideal holiday

Si fuera rico iría a Francia. Tengo ganas de ir el año que viene con mi mejor amiga para unas semanas. Nos alojaríamos en un hotel de cinco estrellas cerca de la playa. Pasaríamos todos los días relajándonos, jugando al tenis, nadando en el mar y tomando el sol. Haríamos nuevos amigos, probaríamos los platos típicos de la región y compraríamos recuerdos. Haría sol todos los días. ¡Qué perfecto!

If I was rich I would go to France. I would like to go next year with my best friend for a few weeks. We would stay in a five-star hotel near the beach. We would spend every day relaxing, playing tennis, swimming in the sea and sunbathing. We would make new friends, we would try the local dishes and buy souvenirs. It would be sunny every day. How perfect!

Ideal weekend

Mi fin de semana ideal sería con mi familia y mis amigos. Si pudiera elegir, iría a Londres para ver un espectáculo con mi madre y al volver a mi casa comeríamos pizza. Si fuera posible pasaríamos el día siguiente haciendo natación y jugando a las cartas. ¡Que relajante!

My ideal weekend would be with my family and my friends. If I could choose, I would go to London to watch a show with my mum and on returning home we would eat pizza.

If it were possible we would spend the following day swimming and playing cards. How relaxing!

Ideal school

Mi colegio ideal sería grande y moderno y estaría cerca de mi casa. Habría un polideportivo, donde pasaríamos muchísimas horas jugando al baloncesto, habría una piscina enorme y un cine. No habría uniforme y los profes no darían deberes durante la semana. Las clases empezarían al mediodía porque según los científicos, los jóvenes necesitan dormir más por la mañana. ¡Qué perfecto!

My ideal school would be big and modern and would be near my house. There would be a sports centre where we would spend many hours playing basketball, an enormous pool and a cinema. There wouldn't be a uniform and the teachers wouldn't give homework during the week. Lessons would begin at midday because according to scientists, young people need more sleep in the morning. How perfect!

What you would change at school

Si pudiera cambiar algo, cambiaría el uniforme porque es incómodo y feo. Estoy harto de él. Tampoco habría deberes durante la semana. Lo importante es que los estudiantes estén totalmente despiertos en clase para que puedan estudiar y aprender. Sería todavía mejor si las clases empezaran más tarde porque, según los científicos, los jóvenes necesitan dormir más por la mañana.

If I could change something, I would change the uniform because it's uncomfortable and ugly. I'm sick of it. Also, there wouldn't be any homework during the week. The important thing is that students are wide awake in class so that they can study and learn. It would be even better if lessons began later because, according to scientists, young people need more sleep in the morning.

What would you do to change your town?

Lo que más me preocupa es que las actividades en mi barrio cuestan un ojo de la cara.

Si pudiera cambiar algo en mi barrio, construiría un centro juvenil para que los jóvenes pudieran reunirse y divertirse sin gastarse un riñón. Además, pondría más rutas para ciclistas porque me encanta el ciclismo y las carreteras son demasiado peligrosas para ciclistas debido al tráfico.

What worries me most is that the activities in my area cost a fortune. If I could change something in my area, I would build a youth centre so that young people could meet up and have fun without having to pay through the nose for it. Also, I would put in more cycle paths because I love cycling and the roads are too dangerous for cyclists due to the traffic.

Ideal job

Si pudiera elegir, y si no tuviera que ganar dinero, iría a un país del tercero mundo para trabajar como médico voluntario. Hay millones de personas que sufren debido a las guerras y al terrorismo y me gustaría hacer algo para ayudarles.

If I could choose and if I didn't have to earn money, I would go to a third world country to do voluntary work as a doctor. There are millions of people suffering because of wars and terrorism and I'd like to do something to help them.

NOTES

Day 8

In this session you will be revising:

- The subjunctive mood
- Vocabulary relating to the environment
- Oral and written answers on environment

The present subjunctive

This is another bonus tense, as in it isn't strictly essential but will catapult you into a new grade bracket if you can shoehorn it into your writing and speaking. It has cropped up earlier in this book in relation to the future tense (with *aunque* and *para que*). It is used after *que* in expressions relating to importance, purpose, negative thinking, emotion and wanting someone to do something.

How to form the subjunctive

To form it, the general rule is that you take the first person singular (the I or yo form) of the present tense, remove the final o and add either an e (if it's an *-ar* verb like *hablar*) or an a (if it's an *-er* or *-ir* verb). I call this vowel swapping. It's as if the verbs are disguising themselves.

habl**o** becomes habl**e**

com**o** becomes com**a**

viv**o** becomes viv**a**

The rest of the verb follows as you'd expect:

Hablar (to speak)	**Comer** (to eat)	**Vivir** (to live)
hable	coma	viva
hables	comas	vivas
hable	coma	viva
hablemos	comamos	vivamos
habléis	comáis	viváis
hablen	coman	vivan

But don't forget that some verbs have unusual *yo* forms

Hago becomes *haga, salgo - salga, pongo - ponga, vengo - venga*

There are 6 irregular subjunctives

dar (to give) - dé

estar (to be) - esté

ser (to be) - sea

ir (to go) - vaya

saber (to know)– sepa

haber (the auxiliary verb that forms the perfect tense) - haya

Use with expressions relating to importance

Es importante que reciclemos – It's important that we recycle.

Use with expressions relating to purpose

Para que mis amigos puedan venir – So that my friends can come

Use with expressions relating to negative thinking

No pienso que **sea** una buena idea – I don't think it's a good idea

Use with expressions relating to emotion

Estoy contenta de que **estés** aquí – I am happy you're here

Use with expressions about wanting someone to do something

Quiere que **haga** mis deberes – S/he wants me to do my homework

Use with cuando in the future

Cuando **sea** mayor, seré profe – When I'm older I'll be a teacher

Use with aunque (although)

Aunque **sea** malo para la salud – Although it's bad for your health

Practise the subjunctive in some good oral / writing sentences

1. I'm going to continue doing sport, although it's tiring, so that I can participate in competitions.
2. I'm going to buy a house in Spain, although it's complicated, so that I can improve my Spanish.
3. I'm going to live in the countryside, although there's no public transport, so that I can breathe more easily.
4. My parents want me to go to university, although it's expensive, so that I can find a job.
5. I don't think it's a good idea.
6. It's important that we make an effort to avoid sugar.
7. I'm happy that my friends are with me.

Answers

1. Voy a seguir haciendo deporte, aunque sea agotador, para que puede participar en concursos.

2. Voy a comprar una casa en España, aunque sea complicado, para que pueda mejorar mi nivel de español.

3. Voy a vivir en el campo, aunque no haya transporte público, para que pueda respirar más fácilmente.

4. Mis padres quieren que vaya a la universidad, aunque sea cara, para que pueda encontrar un trabajo.

5. No pienso que sea una buena idea.

6. Es importante que hagamos un esfuerzo para evitar azúcar.

7. Estoy contento de que mis amigos estén conmigo.

The past subjunctive is used at the beginning of an *if* sentence:

Si pudiera cambiar algo, cambiaría el uniforme.
If I could change something, I would change the uniform.

Si ganara el gordo, compraría una casa.
If I won the lottery, I would buy a house.

Si fuera madre, no sería estricta.
If I were a mother, I wouldn't be strict.

Si tuviera que elegir, viviría en el campo.
If I had to choose, I'd live in the countryside.

NB (and this is a bit advanced!) It is also used just as the present subjunctive is used, when the sentence in question is in the past or the conditional to start with, eg:

Compraría una casa enorme para que mis amigos pudieran visitarme.
I'd buy a huge house so my friends could visit me.

Hice mucho deporte, aunque fuera agotador.
I did lots of sport, although it was tiring.

Estaba contento de que estuviera allí.
I was happy he was there.

To form the past subjunctive, take the *they* form of the preterite (pudieron, ganaron, fueron, tuvieron), and replace the *on* with an *a,* or *an* for plural. Alternatively, just learn the verbs above in the phrases above and try and shoehorn them into your oral or writing somehow.

Vocabulary

el medioambiente	environment
los coches emiten	cars emit
gases tóxicos	toxic gases
las fábricas	factories
los gases suben	the gases rise up
en la atmosfera	into the atmosphere
causan	they cause
la contaminación del aire	air pollution
el calentamiento global	global warming
el efecto invernadero	the greenhouse effect
los mares suben	the sea levels are rising
en peligro	in danger
el problema	the problem
va empeorando	is getting worse
amenazar	to threaten *(menace)*
los vertidos nucleares	nuclear waste
deberíamos	we should
se debe / hay que	it is necessary to
salvar	to save
proteger	to protect
mejorar	to improve
actuar	to act
los recursos naturales	natural resources
agotarse	to run out

What do you do for the environment?

ducharse – me ducho	to shower
para ahorrar agua	to save water
apagar las luces - apago	to turn off the lights
para ahorrar electricidad	to save electricity
reciclar - reciclo	to recycle
el cartón	cardboard
el vidrio y el plástico	glass and plastic
usar - uso	to use
el transporte público	public transport
ir en bici / hacer ciclismo	to cycle
comprar productos ecológicos	to buy green products

Social problems

los sin techo	the homeless *(without a roof)*
dormir en la calle	to sleep rough
duermen	they sleep *(radical changing)*
la pobreza	poverty
el mendigo	beggar *(clothes need mending)*
la inmigración	immigration
los inmigrantes	immigrants
los refugiados	refugees
la falta de dinero	lack of money *(it's a fault)*
la falta de viviendas	lack of housing
sin familias	without families
el paro	unemployment

las drogas	drugs
drogas blandas	soft drugs
piensan que es guay	they think it's cool
a largo plazo	in the long term
las cifras dan miedo	the figures are alarming
recaudar fondos	to raise funds
de segunda mano	secondhand
trabajo voluntario	volunteering

La publicidad	publicity
los anuncios	adverts
las medias	the media
la responsabilidad	responsibility
animar a…. a…	to encourage …. to…
quieren ser	they want to be
más delgado	thinner
más popular	more popular
más guay	cooler
influidos por	influenced by
por todas partes	everywhere
una mala influencia	a bad influence
por muchas razones	for many reasons
nocivo	harmful
informativo	informative
poderoso	powerful
lanzar una campaña	to launch a campaign

| piensan que necesitan | they think they need |
| crear codicia | to create greed |

How much can you remember?

Put two subjunctive expressions in a sentence which also contains a future tense verb.

For your oral and writing

Environment and modern world problems

Standard story for the environment Begin by explaining the main environmental issues (add your own), then explain how you help the environment by imagining taking a shower, turning the light off, going down and taking out the recycling, getting on a bus and shopping for ecological products. In brackets I have put the past tense verbs, and you can use the infinitives to make the future or to say what the government should do.

Environmental problems Los coches y las fábricas producen gases tóxicos que causan la contaminación del aire, el calentamiento global y el efecto invernadero.

Para proteger el medioambiente : Me ducho en vez de bañarme para ahorrar agua (me duché)

- Apago la luz cuando salgo de un cuarto (apagué)
- Reciclo el vidrio, el plástico y el papel (reciclé)
- Uso el transporte público (usé)
- Compro productos ecologicos (compré)

El gobierno debería animar a la gente a (+ infinitives)

Cars and factories produce toxic gases which cause air pollution, global warming and the greenhouse effect. To protect the environment I shower instead of having a bath to save water, I turn off the light when I leave a room, I recycle glass, plastic and paper, I use public transport and I buy ecological products. The government should encourage people to ...

Nowadays what are the biggest environmental problems?

Hoy en día, hay un montón de problemas medioambientales. Lo que más me preocupa es la contaminación. Los coches, las fábricas, y la industria emiten gases tóxicos que suben en la atmosfera y causan la contaminación del aire, el calentamiento global y el efecto invernadero. Por consiguiente, las temperaturas aumentan, se funden los casquetes polares y el nivel de los mares va aumentando. Me da miedo por las generaciones futuras debido a los problemas de calentamiento global.

Nowadays, there are lots of environmental problems. What worries me most is pollution. Cars, factories and industry emit toxic gases, which go into the atmosphere and cause air pollution, global warming and the greenhouse effect. Consequently, the temperatures increase, the polar ice caps melt and the sea level rises. I am afraid for the future generations due to the problems of global warming.

Why protect the environment?

A pesar de nuestros esfuerzos, nuestro planeta está a punto de morir. ¡Qué desastre! Si no hacemos nada, la situación solo empeorará, así que hace falta que todos luchemos por el medioambiente. Es imposible cerrar los ojos ante los problemas asociados con el calentamiento global.

In spite of our efforts, our planet is about to die. What a disaster! If we do not do anything, the situation will only get worse, so we must all fight for the environment. It is impossible to close our eyes to the problems associated with global warming.

What do you do for the environment at school?

En el colegio hacemos todo lo posible para proteger el medioambiente. Hay una papelera de reciclaje en todas las aulas, apagamos las luces cuando salimos de las aulas para ahorrar electricidad y los profesores nos animan a utilizar el transporte público en lugar de un coche para viajar al colegio porque el acto más sencillo puede marcar la diferencia.

At school we do everything possible to protect the environment. There is a recycling bin in every classroom, we turn off the lights when we leave the classrooms to save electricity, and the teachers encourage us to use public transport instead of a car to travel to school, because the simplest act can make a difference.

The causes of poverty in the world

Lo que más me preocupa es la pobreza que se extiende cada vez más, a causa de las guerras, del clima que va cambiando y de los políticos. Las ciudades del mundo están superpobladas, y en poco tiempo habrá grandes problemas de vivienda. Los conflictos mundiales obligan a millones de personas a huir de la hambruna y la persecución. Actualmente, la crisis de refugiados en Europa es una situación humanitaria critica. Incluso en Inglaterra, mucha gente vive por debajo del umbral de la pobreza y la situación va empeorando. El gobierno debería hacer más para ayudar los niños de estas familias para que puedan acceder a la educación y las oportunidades que merecen.

What worries me most is poverty which is becoming more and more widespread because of wars, a changing climate and political conflict. The cities of the world are overpopulated, and in a short time there will be big problems with living space. World conflicts force millions of people to flee hunger and persecution. Currently the refugee crisis in Europe is a critical humanitarian situation. Even in England lots of people live below the poverty line and the situation is getting worse. The government should do more to encourage the children of these families so that they can access the education and the opportunities they deserve.

Importance of the news

Las noticias pueden tener una gran influencia positiva. Son informativas sobre temas actuales y todos tenemos que saber lo que pasa en el mundo. Sin embargo, lo importante es que las noticias sean imparciales, porque los medios son muy poderosos hoy en día.

Es imprescindible que tengamos leyes para que los medios no puedan mentir y manipular a sus lectores, como lo hacen en otros países del mundo.

The news can have a major positive influence. It informs us on current issues and we all need to know what is happening in the world. However, what is important is that the news is unbiased because the media is so powerful today. It is essential that we have laws so that the media cannot lie and manipulate its readers as they do in other countries in the world.

Do you watch the news?

Las noticias me interesan y si tuviera más tiempo, leería un periódico todos los días, pero los profes nos dan demasiados deberes. Tengo la aplicación de la BBC en mi móvil que me avisa cuando pasa algo importante en el mundo, y si quiero saber más, hago clic en el icono para abrirlo.

I am interested in the news and if I had more time I would read a paper every day, but the teachers give us too much homework. I have the BBC app on my phone which tells me when something important happens in the world and if I want to know more, I click on the icon to open it.

What's in the news at the moment?

Los titulares a menudo tratan del medioambiente y del riesgo pandémico debido al coronavirus. En cuanto al medioambiente, hay más terremotos, tormentas e inundaciones que matan a muchísimas personas. El clima está cambiando – no hay duda. Los coches y los aviones emiten gases tóxicos que suben a la atmosfera y causan el calentamiento global y el efecto invernadero. Los mares suben y hay islas que empiezan a desaparecer. Tenemos que actuar antes de que sea demasiado tarde para salvar el planeta.

The headlines are often about the environment and the pandemic risk due to the coronavirus. As far as the environment is concerned, there are more earthquakes, storms and floods which kill a lot of people. The climate is changing – there's no doubt about it. Cars and planes emit toxic gases which go up into the atmosphere and cause global warming and the greenhouse effect. The sea levels are rising and there are islands which are beginning to disappear. We need to act before it's too late to save the planet.

Climate change solution

Tenemos que actuar lo antes posible para salvar el planeta. Tenemos que usar la bici en lugar del coche, viajar menos en avión y ahorrar energía antes de que los recursos naturales se agoten. Deberíamos parar la destrucción de las selvas tropicales que producen el oxígeno que necesitamos. Deberíamos dejar de comer tanta carne porque las vacas tanto como los coches emiten gases tóxicos que causan el cambio climático.

We need to act as soon as possible to save the planet. We need to use bikes instead of the car, travel less by plane and save energy before natural resources run out. We should stop the destruction of tropical rainforests which produce the oxygen we need. We should stop eating so much meat because cows, just like cars, give off toxic gases which cause climate change.

Day 9

In this session you will be revising:

- Weighing up pros and cons
- General vocabulary
- Oral and written answers using pros and cons

Weighing up pros and cons

Lots of exam questions ask you what you think of one thing as opposed to another – do you prefer holidays with friends or family, do you prefer TV or cinema, town or countryside? It's good to have a stock of expressions to put across positive and negative aspects of things:

Positive descriptors

Es más …	it's more…
Hay más …	there are more…
Se puede facilmente	you can easily
No tienes que	you don't have to
Es gratis	it's free
Es barato	it's cheap
Divertido	fun
Simpático	nice
Fácil	easy
Rápido	fast
Bueno para la salud	good for your health
Imprescindible	essential

Negative descriptors

Es menos …..	it's less…
No hay ….	there isn't / aren't any …
No hay suficiente …	there isn't / aren't enough …
Hay menos …	there are less / fewer…
Hay demasiado …	there is too much / there are too many

Hay que / tienes que	you have to
No se puede	you can't
Es caro	it's expensive
Aburrido	boring
Molesto	annoying
Dificil	difficult
Lento	slow
Malo para la salud	bad for your health

Comparisons

If you are asked about your previous school, changes in your school, town or house, or any other comparison question, remember to use the comparing words *más* or *menos, tan* (so / as with adjectives) and *tanto (so much / so many)*. You will also need the imperfect tense rather than the preterite to describe what things used to be like.

About your primary school

Había menos deberes que en mi colegio actual y no teníamos que llegar tan temprano.

There was less homework than in my current school and we didn't have to arrive as early.

About your town

En el pasado teníamos menos rutas para ciclistas y más tiendas. No era tan ruidoso y no había tanta contaminación.

In the past we had fewer cycle paths and more shops. It wasn't as noisy and there wasn't as much pollution.

Test yourself on these

1. My primary school was more fun than my current school
2. There was less homework and more sport
3. We didn't have to wear a uniform
4. In the past it was cleaner but less interesting
5. When I was little I was more sporty
6. There wasn't as much pollution
7. There were fewer cars

Answers

1. Mi escuela primaria era más divertida que mi colegio actual.
2. Había menos deberes y más deporte.
3. No teníamos que llevar uniforme.
4. En el pasado estaba más limpio, pero era menos interesante.
5. Cuando era pequeño, era más deportista.
6. No había tanta contaminación.
7. Había menos coches.

Vocabulary

Prepositions

delante de	in front of
detrás de	behind
encima de	above
en	on or in
debajo de	below
cerca de	near
al lado de	next to
lejos de	far from
a unos minutos de	a few minutes from

Question words

¿Dónde está…?	Where is…?
¿Adónde vas?	Where are you going?
¿De dónde eres?	Where are you from?
¿Quien?	Who?
¿Cuándo?	When?
¿A qué hora?	At what time?
¿Cuál es…?	What / which is…?
¿Qué es…?	What is…?
¿Por qué?	Why…?
¿Cómo…?	How…?
¿Cuántos…?	How many…?

Time

son las dos y media	it's 2.30
son las ocho y cuarto	it's 8.15
son las tres menos cuarto	it's 2.45
es la una menos diez	it's 12.50
a las dos	at 2 o'clock
a la una	at 1 o'clock
al mediodía	at midday
a medianoche	at midnight

Adverbial time phrases and adverbs of time

hoy	today
ayer	yesterday
mañana	tomorrow
la semana pasada	last week
la semana próxima	next week
el año pasado	last year
el año que viene	next year
el año próximo	next year
el fin de semana pasado	last weekend
el fin de semana próximo	next weekend
hace cinco años	5 years ago
en el pasado	in the past
en el futuro	in the future
cuando sea mayor	when I'm older

Frequency

a veces	sometimes
a menudo	often
de vez en cuando	from time to time
siempre	always
todo el tiempo	all the time
todo el día	all day
nunca	never
normalmente	normally
durante la semana	in the week
los fines de semana	at the weekend
tres veces a la semana	three times a week
todos los días	every day
cada día	each day
por la mañana	in the morning
por la tarde	in the afternoon
por la noche	at night
por lo general	in general

Days

lunes	Monday
martes	Tuesday
miércoles	Wednesday
jueves	Thursday
viernes	Friday
sábado	Saturday

domingo	Sunday

Months

Los meses	the months
Hace un mes	a month ago
Durante un mes	for a month
enero	January
febrero	February
marzo	March
abril	April
mayo	May
junio	June
julio	July
agosto	August
septiembre	September
octubre	October
noviembre	November
diciembre	December

Seasons

invierno	winter
primavera	spring
verano	summer
otoño	autumn
las estaciones	the seasons

For your oral and writing

Positives of advertising

La principal ventaja de la publicidad es promover y dar a conocer al público un producto, e informar al consumidor sobre los beneficios que presenta el producto. Es la manera más efectiva de aumentar el número de ventas de un producto, sobre todo hoy en día mediante las redes sociales. Además, aunque pueda ser molesto, la publicidad es la razón por la cual las redes sociales son gratuitas.

The main advantage of advertising is to promote and publicise a product to the public, and to inform the consumer about the benefits. It is the most effective method of increasing the sales of a product, especially today by using social networks. Also, although it can be annoying, advertising is the reason social networks are free.

Negatives of advertising

La publicidad muchas veces nos engaña para que compremos productos o servicios, y puede provocar codicia. Los anuncios que promueven la comida basura y los cigarrillos deberían estar prohibidos porque promueven productos que son malos para la salud y pueden causar enfermedades graves como el cáncer. Además, la publicidad puede tener una influencia peligrosa en los jóvenes que piensan que deberían ser tan delgados y guapos como los modelos que ven en los anuncios, en la tele, donde sea. La presión puede causar trastornos alimentarios como la anorexia.

Advertising often deceives us to make us buy products or services and can provoke greed in people. I think that adverts promoting junk food and cigarettes should be banned because they promote products which are bad for your health and can cause serious illnesses like cancer. Also, advertising can have a dangerous influence on young people who think they should be as thin and gorgeous as the models they see on the adverts, on TV, wherever. The pressure can cause eating disorders like anorexia.

Pros and cons of TV

La televisión puede ser una herramienta educativa y puede ayudar a la gente a descansar y desconectar de la rutina diaria. Es un buen medio de relajarse después de un día estresante en el colegio. Sin embargo, si vemos la televisión, corremos el riesgo de pasar demasiadas horas encerrados en casa. Además, según mucha gente, hay cada vez más violencia en la televisión, particularmente en los dibujos animados que están dirigidos a los niños.

Television can be an educational tool and can help people to rest and disconnect from their daily routine. It is a good way to relax after a stressful day at school. However, if we watch television we risk spending too much time stuck at home. Also, according to many people, there is more and more violence on television, particularly in cartoons aimed at children.

Romantic films v action films

En cuanto al cine, no me gustan nada las películas románticas. Prefiero las películas de acción, sobre todo las pelis de James Bond porque son más emocionantes y no me aburren. Hay un montón de efectos especiales y actuan muchísimas estrellas de cine.

As for cinema, I do not like romantic films at all. I prefer action films, above all James Bond films because they are exciting and they don't bore me. There are loads of special effects and lots of movie stars acting in them.

Cinema or TV?

Prefiero el cine porque a mí me encantan las pelis de ciencia ficción y prefiero verlas en la pantalla grande. Disfruto mucho más de los efectos especiales, de la banda sonora y de los efectos visuales. Además, cuando ves una película en casa, hay un montón de distracciones, y siempre hay alguien que quiere cambiar de canal. Si tuviera más dinero iría todos los días, pero cuesta un ojo de la cara y no puedo permitírmelo.

I prefer the cinema because I love science fiction films and I prefer to watch them on the big screen. I enjoy the effects, the soundtrack and the visual effects much more. Also when you watch a film at home there are loads of distractions and there is always someone who wants to change channel. If I had more money, I'd go every day but it costs an arm and a leg and I can't afford it.

Town v countryside

En mi opinión, la ciudad es mejor que el campo por muchas razones. Por ejemplo, se puede comer en restaurantes, ver películas, ir de compras y reunirse con amigos. Sobre todo, lo que más me gusta es el transporte público, porque no conduzco y tengo que coger el autobús para ir a ver a mis amigos. Si viviera en el campo, no podría ver a mis amigos tan fácilmente. Sin embargo, hay ventajas de vivir en el campo. Es más tranquilo que la ciudad, es más relajante y se puede pasear al aire libre. En la ciudad, lo que más me preocupa es el tráfico y la contaminación del aire que van empeorando.

In my opinion the city is better than the countryside for many reasons. For example, you can eat in restaurants, watch films, go shopping and meet up with friends. What I like most is the public transport because I don't drive and I have to take the bus to go and see my friends. If I lived in the countryside I wouldn't be able to see my friends so easily. However, there are advantages of living in the countryside. It is quieter than the city, it's more relaxing and you can walk in the fresh air. In the city what bothers me most is the traffic and air pollution which are getting worse.

Is marriage important or not?

No importa si estás casado o no, sobre todo porque tantos matrimonios fracasan, y el número de personas solteras crece. Muchos niños son testigos de divorcio y viven con hermanastros y hermanastras. No sé si voy a casarme o no. Me gustaría vivir con alguien durante unos años antes de tomar una decisión tan importante. Deberíamos aprender más sobre las relaciones en el colegio para que sepamos lo que supone el matrimonio.

It doesn't matter if you are married or not, especially because so many marriages break down and the number of single people is increasing. Lots of children have witnessed divorce and live with step-brothers and step-sisters. I don't know if I will get married or not. I'd like to live with someone for a few years before making such an important decision. We should learn more about relationships at school so that we know what marriage involves.

Holidays with family or friends

Aunque sea gratis ir de vacaciones con la familia, prefiero viajar con amigos porque es más divertido y tenemos más libertad. Podemos salir por la noche sin tener que pedir permiso. No hay que visitar museos aburridos y se puede comer comida basura en lugar de verduras.

Although it's free to go on holiday with your family, I prefer to travel with friends because it's more fun and we have more freedom. We can go out at night without having to ask permission. You don't have to visit boring museums and you can eat junk food instead of vegetables.

Day 10

In this session you will be revising:

- How to produce a good essay using the writing mnemonic
- How to approach the listening exam
- Synonyms and homonyms

The writing mnemonic...

Leave a line so you can add things later to increase word count.

Modals

The verbs to have to, to be able to, to want to are all modal verbs and you need to show the examiner that you can use them in all tenses

Tuve que volver a casa	I had to
Deberíamos proteger el medioambiente	We should protect
Se puede hacer deporte	One can do
Quiero ser abogado	I want to be

Negatives

No tengo animales	I don't have
No me gusta el queso	I don't like
Nunca voy al cine	I never go

Opinions

En mi opinión	In my opinion
Creo que	I believe
Pienso que	I think
Me parece que	It seems to me that

Pronouns

Los profes nos dan	The teachers give us
Me levanto	I get up

Lo encuentro fácil	I find it easy
Estudiándolo	studying it

Qué

¡Qué desastre!	What a disaster!
¡Qué pena!	What a pain!
¡Qué suerte!	How lucky!
¡Qué delicioso!	How delicious!
¡Qué pesadilla!	What a nightmare!

Reasons

Porque, puesto que, dado que	because
Debido a	due to

Superlatives (and comparatives)

El mejor colegio de Londres	The best school in London
Es más deportista que yo	S/he is more sporty than me

Time phrases

Antes de + infinitive	before (doing something)
Después de + infinitive	After (doing something)
Al llegar	On arriving
Acabo de	I have just

Dos veces a la semana	Twice a week
A las cinco de la tarde	At five o'clock in the afternoon
Todos los días	Every day
Bastante a menudo	Quite often

Umbrella (weather!)

Hizo sol	It was hot
Llueve / nieva	It is raining / snowing
Llovía / nevaba	It was raining / snowing
Llovió / nevó	It rained / snowed
Hacía buen tiempo	The weather was good

Verbs

Use all the tenses you can possibly cram in:

Present	eg. hago mucho deporte
Preterite	eg. hizo sol
Imperfect	eg. cuando era pequeño
Perfect	eg. he visitado muchos países
Near Future	eg. voy a ir al cine
Future simple	eg. iremos al teatro
Past subjunctive	eg. si fuera rico
Conditional	eg. compraría una casa
Present subjunctive	eg. es importante que haga sol

Top tips for the listening

Do as many papers as you can and learn vocabulary!

Each exam board has a slightly different question style. Using the exam board website, do as many past papers as possible and check your answers using the mark scheme. Students who know the most vocab get the highest marks.

Use the reading time

Use every second of the preparation time you are given to assess what you need to be listening out for. In the more complex comprehension passages, it is a good idea to know what to listen out for before the passage starts playing and will make the listening task less stressful.

Don't write and listen at the same time

Believe it or not, actual multitasking is pretty much impossible. Girls and women tend to be better at switching between tasks quickly, but don't rely on writing your answers at the same time as listening to the audio. Imagine you're listening to a friend talking – you don't need to write everything down then do you? Think of this exercise as similar to that. If you have read the questions and can develop a code for notes (see below) then the rest of the work is just building a picture in your mind of what is being said, just as you would do when listening to a friend.

Practise writing notes

Even if you don't manage to do full practice papers, you can listen to the radio, to recordings on exam websites or on BBC Bitesize, and practise making notes using symbols and abbreviations that don't take up valuable time. For example, a big pound / dollar sign might mean expensive, and a small one cheap. You can draw arrows to indicate travel, and numbers are quick to write when it comes to dates, room numbers and ages. After listening to a few tracks from previous papers you will see how the same themes recur and you can develop your own code system to represent the words you hear.

Look out for negatives and superlatives

They will be trying to trip you up, you can bet on it. Watch out for words like *nunca, tampoco, nadie, ningun,* which will change the meaning of the sentence entirely. Similarly, someone might talk about what they like using *me gusta* but if they end up saying *prefiero (I prefer)* or *sobre todo (most of all)* then that is the thing they like most and that will be your answer.

You don't need to understand every word

There is always going to be the odd word you don't know. Don't panic. Part of the exercise is using your initiative to work out what words and phrases mean from the context you find them in. For example, you might hear this:

Los documentales pueden ser una herramienta educativa

What does *herramienta* mean? Well, the sentence means "documentaries can be an educational *something*"

Does it matter what it means? Probably not, because the thing is, you have the gist here – basically that documentaries are educational.

Herramienta means *tool* by the way, in case you were wondering!

Synonyms for the listening paper

A key element to doing well in the listening is vocabulary. To have a chance of getting a good mark, you will need to have a good grasp of the word lists set out at the back of this book. However, it is in this part of the exam that you need to be aware of more than one Spanish word for the English – so for example, there are at least three words for "job" along with associated adjectives. Good knowledge of synonyms is essential to your success, so I have grouped some of the main words you need below, in categories relating to their meaning. They have been taken from past papers over the last four years or so.

Work and employment

This topic comes up very frequently. It's important that you know and recognise all the different words for work, job, company and pay. Watch out for *poco* because it means *little* but with a negative connotation – as in *not very much*.

Trabajo	work, job
Empleo	job
Carrera	career
Laboral	work (adjective)
Experiencia laboral	work experience
Trabajador	hardworking
Una compañía	company
Una empresa	a company. enterprise
El sueldo	salary
La paga	pay
Ganar dinero	to earn money
Gano poco	I don't earn much
La huelga	strike

School and education

La escuela	school
El insti(tuto)	school
Escolar	school (adjective)
La comida escolar	school dinners
Estudios	studies, schoolwork

Estudiar	to study
Estudiantes	students
Enseñar	to teach
La enseñanza	education
Lenguas	languages
Los idiomas	languages
Extranjeros	foreign

Necessity

Tengo que	I have to
Hay que	it is necessary / one must
Necesito	I need
Debería	I / S/he, it should
Obligatorio	compulsory
Hace falta	it is necessary
Prohibido	prohibited
Optativo	optional

Health

Comida means lunch as well as food, and *alimentos* also means food, which should remind you of the alimentary canal.

La salud	health
Saludable	healthy
Sano	healthy

Poco saludable	unhealthy
El ocio	leisure
Actividades	activities
Enfermo	ill
Enfermedad	illness
Enfermero/-a	nurse
Me duele la cabeza	my head hurts
El dolor	pain
El médico	doctor
Mejor	better
Mejorar	to improve
La comida	food OR lunch
Alimentos	food
Comida basura	junk food
Comida rápida	fast food
Alimentos grasos	fatty food
El azúcar	sugar
Azucarado	sweet
Dulce	sweet
Los dulces	sweet things
Caramelos	sweets
La ensalada	salad
Sabroso	tasty

El sabor	flavour
Delicioso	delicious
Rico	tasty (food) OR rich (money)
Asqueroso	disgusting
Postre	pudding

Ll words

English students famously muddle all the Spanish words beginning with Ll. Here are the most common ones that tend to confuse:

Llevar	to wear
Llevo un uniforme	I wear a uniform
Llevarse bien	to get on
Nos llevamos bien	we get on well
Llegar	to arrive
La llegada	arrival
Llueve	it's raining
Llovió	it rained
Llovía	it was raining
La lluvia	rain

Prices

I have yet to find a listening exam which doesn't mention the cost of things, so make sure you're aware of all the ways this can appear:

| Caro | expensive |

Precios altos	high prices
Precios bajos	low prices
Costar	to cost
Cuesta mucho	it costs a lot
De alto coste	expensive
Costoso	costly
Cuesta poco	it doesn't cost much
Barato	cheap
De bajo coste	cheap
Gratis	free

Positive reactions

You will need to know all the different ways of expressing likes and dislikes, and associated phrases which imply liking or disliking:

Me gusta	I like (it)
Me gustan	I like (them)
Le gusta	S/he likes (it)
Le gustan	S/he likes (them)
Les gusta	They like (it)
Les gustan	They like (them)
Me encanta	I love
Cómico	funny
Gracioso	funny
Divertido	fun

Divertirse	to have fun
Disfrutar	to enjoy
Me hace reír	it makes me laugh
Me hace sonreír	it makes me smile
Me hace feliz	it makes me happy
Me pone contento	it makes me happy
Me hace sentirme bien	it makes me feel good
Me da energía	it gives me energy
Me dan energía	they give me energy
De mis sueños	of my dreams
Un placer	a pleasure
Pasarlo bien	to have a good time
Pasarlo mal	to have a bad time
Lo pasé bomba	I had a great time
Mejor	better
Mejorar	to improve

Negative reactions

Difícil / duro	hard
Odio	I hate
Asqueroso	disgusting
Aburrido	boring
Molesto	annoying

Aburrirse	to get bored
Monótono	boring, monotonous
Me cuesta	I find it hard
Lo encuentro duro	I find it hard
Peor / empeorar	worse / to get worse
Decepcionado	disappointed
Me fastidia / molesta	it annoys me

Time and routine

Knowing when and how often someone does something can be critical to getting the answer right.

La rutina	routine
La vida cotidiana	daily life
Todos los días	every day
Todo el día	all day
Siempre	always
A veces	sometimes
de vez en cuando	sometimes, from time to time
Una vez al mes	once a month
Dos veces a la semana	twice a week
Muchas veces	often
A menudo	often
Nunca	never
Suelo salir	I usually go out

Con retraso	delayed
Tarde	late
Temprano	early

Walking

Ir a pie	to go on foot
Ir andando	to walk
Andar	to walk
Caminar	to walk
Dar un paseo	to go for a walk
Dar una vuelta	to go for a walk / ride

The *que* sound

This sounds like *kay* and not only means *what which* or *than*, but is the beginning of a few commonly misunderstood words:

Quedarse	to stay / remain
Me quedo	I stay
Me quedé	I stayed
Quejarse	to complain
Se quejan	they complain
Quemar	to burn
Quemado	burnt
Querer	to want / love
Querido	dear, loved

Queso	cheese

Something and nothing, up and down, success and failure

Here are a few words that can drastically change the meaning of a sentence:

Algo	something
Algunos casos	some cases
Nunca	never
Nada	nothing
Ningún	no
Tampoco	neither
Nadie	nobody
Cualquier	any
Aumentar	to go up, increase
El aumento	the increase
Subir	to go up
Tener éxito	to succeed
Disminuir	to go down
Bajar	to lower, get out of
Ha bajado	it has gone down
Suspender	to fail
Sacar un suspenso	to fail

Starting and stopping

Empezar	to begin
Comenzar	to begin, commence
Al principio	at the beginning
Parar	to stop
Pararse	to stop (oneself)
El autobús se paró	the bus stopped
Acabar	to stop or to have just
Acabo de llegar	I have just arrived
Dejar de fumar	to stop smoking

Past participles

These often bear no relation to the verb itself, so learn to recognise where they come from.

He dicho (from decir)	I have said
Han hecho (from hacer)	They have done
Has vuelto (from volver)	You have returned
Ha visto (from ver)	S/he has seen
Habéis puesto (from poner)	You (pl) have put / laid
Ha muerto (from morir)	S/he has died
Hemos roto (from romper)	We have broken
Ha sido (from ser)	It has been
Un hecho	A fact

Gerunds

The *-ing* in English words usually corresponds to *ando* or *iendo* in Spanish ones, but sometimes where the infinitive is short, as in *ser, ver, ir, dar,* you end up with more ending than verb, which can be disconcerting!

Viendo	watching
Dando	giving
Yendo	going
Siendo	being
Va empeorando	it's getting worse
Va mejorando	it's getting better
Seguir estudiando	to carry on studying

Preterites

As with the gerunds above, some preterite forms bear little resemblance to the original infinitive:

Hice	I did / made
Hizo	S/he did / made
Hizo sol	it was sunny
Hicieron	they did / made
Puse	I put (past)
Puso	S/he put
Pusieron	They put
Tuve	I had
Tuvo	S/he had

Hubo	There was (occurred)
Pude	I was able to
Pudo	S/he was able to
Pudieron	They were able to
Fui	I went
Fue	S/he went / was
Fueron	They were / went
Dije	I said / told
Dijo	S/he said / told
Di	I gave
Dio	S/he gave
Dieron	They gave
Estuve	I was (in a place)
Estuvo	S/he was (in a place)
Estuvieron	They were (in a place)
Vine	I came
Vino	S/he came
Vinieron	They came

P words

Pelirrojo	red-haired
Peligroso	dangerous
Película	film
Peluquero	hairdresser

Peluquería	hairdresser's shop
Pelearse	to fight
Perezoso	lazy

Numbers

Trece	13
Treinta	30
Cincuenta	50
Quinientos	500
Cinco	5
Quince	15
Catorce	14
Cuatro	4
Cuarenta	40

Heat

El calor	heat
Caliente	hot
El calentamiento global	global warming
La calefacción	heating
Caluroso	warm

Tener expressions

Tener éxito	to succeed
Tener razón	to be right
Tener ganas de	to want to
Tener hambre	to be hungry
Tener sed	to be thirsty
Tener miedo	to be afraid

There is and it is – and their variations

Hay	there is / there are
Había	there was / there were
Habrá	there will be
Habría	there would be
Es	it is
Era / fue	it was
Será	it will be
Sería	it would be

How much can you remember?

What is the writing mnemonic? Give examples of each one.

The ten most common mistakes – don't make them!

1. **Adjective agreements**
   I guarantee you will miss some – please prove me wrong! Take care especially when the adjective comes a long way after the noun, eg: *las fiestas en España son frecuentes y mucho más conocidas que en Inglaterra.*

2. **Liking**
   A mi amiga le gusta el chocolate – remember all components of a liking phrase, use the *a* if you're identifying the person, use the right pronoun and an article before the thing they like. Same goes for *me interesa, me fascina* etc.

3. **Infinitives**
   After *me gusta* (and other likes / dislikes), *para, suelo, tengo que, voy a, es importante, puedo, se puede, decidir* – use an infinitive.

4. **Ser and estar**
   Ser is for characteristics, *estar* is for positions, emotions and temporary states.

5. **Ing**
   Don't use gerunds (*-ando* and *-iendo*) wherever you find the -ing in English. Use them with *estar* (estoy estudiando), with *paso mucho tiempo* (charlando) and *seguir* (to continue).

6. **Personal a**
   Remember with helping and encouraging you need an *a* before the person (ayuda a mis padres / animar a la gente a).

7. **You don't play sport**
   You do it. Hago mucho deporte.

8. **You play *al* futbol**
   Easy to use el instead, it seems!

9. **Para not por**
   Most people overuse *por* – if in doubt it is probably *para*, which means in order to (with a verb) or for (with a person or noun).

10. **Si pudiera cambiar algo, cambiaría…**
    This is your go-to sentence for the conditional, when talking about what you'd change in school, town, house etc – use it!

Other publications also available on Amazon:

How to Ace your French oral

How to Ace your Spanish oral

How to Ace your German oral

French vocabulary for GCSE

Spanish vocabulary for GCSE

The French GCSE handbook

The Spanish GCSE handbook

Advanced French Conversation

A level French Vocabulary

The A level French handbook

The Common Entrance French Handbook

Brush up your French – a revision guide for grown-ups

Ten Magic tricks with French

Spanish in a week

Countdown to French GCSE

If you have any comments or questions on any of the content of this book, please do get in touch via my website: www.lucymartintuition.co.uk. Find me on Facebook and like my page to be first in the running for news and offers and free books. And for some extra tips on how to impress examiners with your oral and writing, subscribe to my Lucy Martin Tuition YouTube channel.

Printed in Great Britain
by Amazon